0281054134 3 048 OF

The Reverend Giles Legood is a Church of England priest who is working as a university chaplain in the Diocese of London. In his present post and previously in parish ministry, he has conducted hundreds of funerals and worked with people in their bereavement. He has edited *Chaplaincy: The Church's Sector Ministries* and *Veterinary Ethics: An Introduction*.

Professor Ian Markham is the Dean of Hartford Seminary, Connecticut, USA, and is also a Visiting Professor of Theology at Liverpool Hope University College. He has taught theology and religious studies to university students, ordination candidates, church groups and others for many years. He has written *Truth and the Reality of God* and co-edited *September 11: Religious Perspectives on the Causes and Consequences*.

The authors met as students at King's College, London and together have previously produced *The Godparents' Handbook* and *The Church Wedding Handbook*, both published by SPCK.

D1355461

Also by the same authors

The Godparents' Handbook, 1997, SPCK
The Church Wedding Handbook, 2000, SPCK

THE FUNERAL HANDBOOK

GILES LEGOOD
and
IAN MARKHAM

First published in Great Britain in 2003 by
Society for Promoting Christian Knowledge
Holy Trinity Church
Marylebone Road
London NW1 4DU

Copyright © Giles Legood and Ian Markham 2003

All rights reserved. No part of this book may be reproduced or
transmitted in any form or by any means, electronic or
mechanical, including photocopying, recording, or by any
information storage and retrieval system, without permission in
writing from the publisher.

Bible quotations are from the *New Revised Standard Version
of the Bible*, copyright © 1989 by the Division of Christian Education
of the National Council of the Churches of Christ in the USA.
Used by permission. All rights reserved.

British Library Cataloguing-in-Publication Data
A catalogue record for this book is available from
the British Library

ISBN 0–281–05413–4

1 3 5 7 9 10 8 6 4 2

Typeset by Pioneer Associates, Perthshire
Printed in Great Britain by
The Cromwell Press, Trowbridge, Wiltshire

LEICESTER CITY LIBRARIES	
0281054134 3 048 0F	
Cypher	20.06.03
393.90882	£8.99

To the communities of

The Parish of Holy Cross, Bearsted
and
Hartford Seminary, Connecticut

Contents

Introduction

'In this world nothing can be said to be certain except death and taxes.' While many might try hard to minimize the latter, none of us can avoid the former. Death is the one human experience that we can all anticipate with absolute certainty. It is amazing, therefore, that so many people are nervous about talking of death and will do all they can to avoid mentioning the dreaded 'd' word. The authors of this book believe that it is good and healthy to talk about death and dying in the same way that it is good and healthy to talk about some of the other things in life that unite all of humanity: love and relationships.

We would not, however, want to encourage people to be too concerned with thinking about their death and the death of others (obsessiveness with any subject or idea is rarely a good thing). Nevertheless, we do believe that thinking through some of the issues and choices that have to be made around the time of death, both by those who are dying and those who care for them, is a good and useful thing to do. There are many big decisions that need to be made at this time and it is surely better that such decisions are made after considered reflection, thought and prayer than made quickly, with little time for consideration of the various issues, 'on the hoof'. It is hoped that this book will be useful to those thinking through what, if anything, they would like to be done to remember them after their own death, as well those who will need a helpful written guide in make decisions on behalf of another after the other's death. In addition, the book should serve the clergy and others in the caring professions who may find it helpful to place this book into the hands of such people as an introduction and aid to negotiate the choices that will have to be faced around the time of death.

The book is intended both to be dipped into to answer specific questions which our readers might have and to be read through systematically, raising points for further thought, consideration and action. We hope that readers will take from the book what is useful to them in their own particular circumstances and lay the rest aside, as is most appropriate. We do not claim that the book is to be seen as the final word on the subject of funerals but it is written out of our experience of handling bereavement, both personally and professionally. In our current jobs and in previous working environments we have walked alongside many going through sad times as we have taught theology and offered pastoral care. In this project, as in much else in life, truth is what works.

Sadly, many of those who have taught us much and shown us real love are no longer with us. We do count ourselves fortunate, however, to have been blessed by the lives of those we have loved whom we see no longer and by the lives of our families and friends who surround us today. Their lives, like ours, have been touched and blessed by countless special people who have died. All of these experiences have generally helped us in the writing of this book. Specifically, however, we are enormously grateful to Lesley Markham, whose professional expertise contributed so significantly to the discussion of financial issues which is the subject of Chapter 5; to Keith Arrowsmith whose legal brain was consulted in this and previous writing projects; and to Yvonne Bowen-Mack and Gwyn Jervis for some much appreciated everyday help and friendship.

Finally, we should like to dedicate this book to two communities that have given us much in various ways. One community has sustained one of the authors since birth, setting him on the way and teaching him an immeasurable amount about human life and the Christian faith, while the second has, in much more recent times, taken the other author to another stage on his Christian journey and offered an example of how that faith can be enriched by contact with believers from other faith communities. Both have given and will continue to give us much to be thankful for.

CHAPTER ONE

Coping with Death

It was Benjamin Franklin who stated that: 'In this world nothing can be said to be certain except death and taxes.' Today there is an entire industry devoted to worrying about taxes. Newspapers dedicate many column inches to the problem and thousands are employed in either the collection or avoidance of taxes. Oddly professions concerned with death are much smaller businesses. Churches, of course, take an interest in death, but funeral directors (with some notable US exceptions) are often small family firms, and very little space in newspapers and magazines is given over to the issues surrounding death.

Although understandable, such priorities are probably unhealthy. Our attitudes towards death are understandable because few people want to pay even more of their hard-earned income to the Government and few want to think about their mortality. But such avoidance is unhealthy because our lack of thought about death makes us so unprepared when it inevitably strikes. Coping with the death of others needs thought. Coping with the idea of our own death also needs serious thought. We need to prepare ourselves for these inevitabilities. A prepared life, aware of the certainty that everyone we value will one day cease to be, is a life that appreciates the present moment so much more. It can and should generate a healthy disposition to life.

Naturally this is not always the case. It is possible to be morbidly preoccupied with death, to take endless fascination in the end of life. As with all questions, a sense of balance and perspective is needed. In the same way as the enjoyment of travel can be distorted by a preoccupation with the possibility of accidents, so the enjoyment of life can be distorted by an obsessive attention to mortality.

The appropriate attitude then is one of balance. In this book we want to explore the reality of death, yet to do so in a way that makes it a constructive part of our lives. For Christians, facing such a reality is part of our calling. We are called to recognize the reality of death, not as the termination of everything that we value, but as a necessary precursor to the growth that God has made possible through eternal life. We are also called to judge our lives in the light of death. It is often the case that people who discover that they have only a limited, and known, time to live (for example, having to cope with a terminal illness) often then realize how much their lives are cluttered up with trivial, incidental preoccupations. The next episode of *Coronation Street*, important though it is, is definitely less important than a relationship with your children or your partner. Often when we are consciously forced to recognize the limited nature of human life this insight comes into sharp focus.

In life we have to cope with death in two major ways. The first is the death of other people. There are some people, for instance, who are picking up this book aware that someone close to them is about to die or perhaps has just died. This might be the first of several times when they will have to cope with the death of someone else. The second major way of having to cope with death is coping with our own death. It might be said that the good thing about our own death is that we, at least, do not have to cope with that tragic sense of loss. However, there comes a time in all our lives when we can start to see changes in our bodies, which makes us think about the end of life. Perhaps we are aware that we are unlikely to experience a certain date in the future. Exactly how close that date is to the present time often depends on our age. Those in middle age (from the age of 40 or so) are unlikely to be around in 60 years from now. For those in young old age (say, 70 or so), 20 years from now will see many changes: changes in mobility, independence, and perhaps health. In the rest of this chapter we shall briefly look at how we 'cope' with these aspects of death.

Coping with the death of others

All people are born into a complex network of relationships. At birth, we find ourselves surrounded by parents, perhaps brothers and sisters, and perhaps grandparents, uncles and aunts. Due to the fact we are social animals, as we grow up we spend much of our time developing friendships. We learn, from childhood onwards, the importance of sharing. We find some people whom we like and others whom we find harder to like. With those we like we laugh, smile, share common interests and look forward to seeing each other. With those we find harder to like, our relationships develop less easily or positively. At their extreme, the latter relationships can be characterized by hate, anger and hostility.

All these relationships define us. If you ask the question 'Who am I?' part of the answer will involve the network of relationships that endlessly shape you. To such a question we reply, 'I am the daughter of my parents' or 'I am the father of my child.' Outside family structures, even when we define ourselves around our work, relationships with others are implicit. For example, a response such as 'I am an accountant' implies clients, colleagues and a boss. When we think about who we are, we find ourselves thinking about relationships with other people.

It is this network of relationships that can make death so significant. Death means that a person around whom many significant relationships exist is no longer with us. There is a significant gap: a link in our network of relationships has disappeared. The extent of that loss ripples out from those most significant to those less significant. With few exceptions, for every person who dies there is a parent, partner or child who is devastated. There are friends who find their social lives reconfigured and the loss of a quality or type of friendship (for all friendships have their own distinctive quality). Those who knew the person in a professional capacity will also be losing a colleague. At lots of different levels the departed link might provoke ambiguous feelings. Certain relationships are not positive. There are husbands who batter their wives. There are friends who can be draining and destructive of healthy living. There are bosses at work who are unreasonable and unkind to their employees. In these cases the death of such a person may well provoke very mixed emotions.

In all cases of coping with the death of others it is important to stress that there is an overwhelming complexity about the loss of a significant person in your life. Acknowledging the complexity of the loss is a good place to start. The most basic lesson about coping that needs to be learnt is that naming and expressing your feelings is vitally important. Shock and disbelief are common starting points. Anger and guilt often follow. In all cases, the feelings need to be identified and expressed.

This is not a book about bereavement. You will find in the Useful Addresses section at the end of this book lots of suggestions for helping with these feelings. The focus of this book is the contribution that the Church can make to coping with death (both that of others and your own) and the practicalities surrounding this. However, it is worth briefly looking at the various stages of bereavement, which many experience in their grief.

Many thinkers and writers on bereavement outline seven stages, which are typically undergone in bereavement. These stages do not necessarily occur chronologically nor do they necessarily all occur. Each individual will react to grief in different ways and will cope according to their own personality and needs. Nevertheless the stages, such as they are, are set out for you to consider. The first stage involves a sense of shock and numbness. This is at its most intense right at the outset of hearing of the death and typically can last from a few minutes to several hours. The second stage involves denial where the bereaved person cannot quite believe that the person has actually died. The third stage is anger where anger is felt by the bereaved that the deceased person has left them. The fourth stage is a sense of guilt. This guilt can involve a sense that there is something that the bereaved person could have done to prevent the death or, more commonly, a sense that there were certain things that needed to be said or unsaid or done or undone. The fifth stage is bargaining. This stage is especially pertinent for those who are religious – the religious person will attempt to bargain with God. The sixth stage is a depression, which may occur when the bereaved person comes to terms with the long-term loss of a significant relationship. The final stage is acceptance. It is important to stress that this stage does not mean one is 'back to normal'. Things will never be the same again and there is a sense in which you never get over the loss of someone close to you, as a significant relationship in your network has gone forever. However, you do reach an accommodation with this changed world. This is acceptance.

Funerals are often an important way for the process of grieving to be helped. Handled properly, they can help progress towards the acceptance stage. How this is best done will be a theme of later chapters.

Coping with your own death

The other potential reader of this book is the person who is increasingly aware of her or his own mortality and wants to make a few preparations. We have already noted that it is both commendable and appropriate to recognize that one day our time on earth will end. This need not be a morbid thought. It is simply facing facts. However, as we reflect further on this fact, we need to recognize that facing such a thought is complicated.

It is, of course, possible that we might die at any moment. Spend an evening listening to the national news and one becomes aware of the tens or hundreds of people who started the morning that day believing that they had a future, only to have their lives tragically terminated. Traffic accidents, natural disasters, murders and other things besides can 'unnaturally' terminate human life. It is right for us to recognize this possibility, but it is also important that we think about this possibility in the light of what is probable. The percentage of people who wake up and who then have their lives ended during the day due to some disaster or misfortune is very small. Television and newspapers mostly report only the important or unusual. Truly representative national news would be very boring indeed. Each day the vast majority of people will get up, do a day's work, come home and go to bed. The authors of this book know well the cities of Liverpool and London (two relatively dangerous cities). Most human lives that are lived in these cities are uneventful, however – nothing spectacular happens. A healthy recognition of the possibility of a tragic termination of life is right and proper but it is important to keep it in perspective.

The reason why this recognition is healthy is that it is important that we ensure that if our life ended today we would feel that everything important to us is correctly ordered. By this we mean that we are happy with our network of relationships. Sadly sometimes the combination of pride and misunderstanding can damage even very significant relationships. There are parents who are not talking to their children and there are children who are not talking to their siblings (television shows such as *Oprah* would soon come off the air if this were not so). In the New Testament, Jesus explains why it is important to make sure that relationships are sorted out before coming to God to repent of one's sins:

> So when you are offering your gift at the altar, if you remember that your brother or sister has something against you, leave your gift there before the altar and go; first be reconciled with your brother or sister, and then come and offer your gift. (Matthew 5.23–4)

Here Jesus is stressing the need for 'ordered relationships'. Trying to make sure that 'the sun does not go down on your wrath' is a good principle. This means trying to finish every day with your significant relationships intact and healthy (however infuriating other people might be at times).

Ensuring that in the event of untimely demise our relationships with others are healthy is one aspect of coping with our own death. However, another aspect is that felt by those who are elderly as they approach the end of life. As humans move into their eighties and nineties they naturally become much more aware of the precious nature of time and the inevitability of death.

Sadly we live in a culture that does not esteem the elderly. In other parts of the world, the lifetime of wisdom which can be accumulated by the elderly gives them an entitlement to respect. The Jewish book of teachings, the Talmud, instructs the young to always stand up in the presence of the elderly. In contrast, however, Western culture too often simply celebrates youth to the exclusion of all else. Images on advertising hoardings stress the importance of youth and of remaining young-looking. The elderly are exhorted to make way for the young. It can be very difficult for someone in their fifties to find a job. Ageism (the irrational discrimination against people simply because they are older) is alive and well.

Recognition that we are in an unsympathetic culture towards ageing is an important one as we consider death and dying. Sending out firm signals that as people grow old they are still able to think, make decisions and enjoy life is important. It is a common feature of growing old to distinguish between our physical age and the age we feel. Even though we know that our mobility is less good and trips to the bathroom in the night are more frequent, elderly people often talk of still feeling as if they were 21 inside. They do not feel that they have changed. It is important that young and old alike recognize that this is the case. The appearance of age should not mislead people. There is often a young person's mind inside an elderly body.

Along with these important messages that need to be acknowledged by all there are also other important messages that need to be received. The network of relationships changes as ageing moves on. The chances are that, in the passing of time, the children have left home, the parent has become a grandparent, the adjustment from working to retirement has had to be handled and the anxieties about care when one is very old need to be faced.

It is worth giving significant reflection to these areas because 'coping with our own death' is largely a matter of ensuring that our relationships with those around us are life-enhancing rather than difficult, and being aware that changes in role often create major difficulties for those who are elderly. One example of change in the order of relationships is that of parent to child on the arrival of grandchildren.

Relationships with grandchildren are for most people a complete delight. Grandparents are not required to be the primary disciplinarians of the child but instead are permitted to gently 'spoil' and 'indulge' the grandchild. Where on a day-to-day basis the relationship with the parent will go up and down, the grandparent can remain in the background sending out positive and supportive signals. It is often not the relationships with grandchildren themselves that cause problems for grandparents but rather it is the relationship with the parents (the son or daughter and of course the son-in-law and the daughter-in-law). Such an example shows us that one of the privileges of old age is that often an elderly person is someone who is able to enjoy more freedom than at any other time of their life.

The shocking death

Before we finish this chapter a brief word needs to be addressed to the person who is suffering the loss of a young child or a premature and sudden loss of partner or other loved one. All death is shocking (even the most expected) but some can be especially devastating. In some cases the shock of the death can be almost overwhelming.

A premature death always seems so unjust. Parents expect their children to outlive them. Husbands and wives most often marry expecting to share old age with each other. To have these lives and expectations suddenly cut short is very difficult. More often than not, there is no short cut to being able to 'get over' such deaths. The grief and pain, which will be considerable, must be simply lived through. The space to weep, rage and pray is essential. In the short term, the goal will simply be to cope. Awareness of the extent of the pain is the key to coping with the death that is unexpected (as it is with other death too). One should never underestimate how much healing there will need to be.

Yet a 'good funeral' (and yes, the phrase is deliberately odd) can be an important part of the healing process. You will need to try to take control of as much as you can. Involve yourself in the details of the planning of the funeral. Make sure the 'send-off' is appropriate to you, although recognize too that you will be one person among many who is hurting deeply.

Embarking on this book

Thus far we have tried to meet readers of this book wherever they are at. You might be reading this book sensitive to the friend or relative who has died and therefore you need help to arrange the funeral. You might equally be reading this book because you are aware of the nearing inevitability of death (either your own or that of another person). Whatever position you find yourself in, part of the secret of a happy life is to accept the global and universal reality that human life is finite.

Prayer for those who have recently lost a loved one

God our Creator, who brought us to birth and in whose arms we die, comfort us all who mourn the loss of (*name*). Embrace us with your tender love, give us hope for new life in the days and weeks ahead and help us see that with you nothing is

11

wasted or incomplete. This we ask in the name of him who died for us, Jesus Christ, your Son, our Lord. Amen.

Prayer for those who are aware of growing old

Eternal God, who through the ages remains the same, be near to me as I grow old. Though my body fails, let my mind be strong and my faith in you endure, so that with patience I may bear all things, believe all things, hope all things, endure all things and at the last may meet death unafraid, through Jesus Christ our Lord. Amen.

Prayer for those in a state of shock

O God, you rule over your creation with tenderness, offering fresh hope in the midst of the most terrible misery. We pray for all those whose souls are blackened by despair. Infuse them with the pure light of your love, shower on them your gentleness that even in their darkest moments they may be open to your love and bring kindness to one another and to themselves. Amen.

CHAPTER TWO

Funerals and Death

In Chapter 1 we looked at the themes of ageing and death. In this chapter we shall start to explore the relationship of death and dying to the funeral (this is, after all, *The* Funeral *Handbook*). There is a long and complicated history to this relationship so we start with a brief history of various rites that surround death. After this we shall go global and look at the different ways in which the transition from death to life has been marked. The next part of this chapter will then consider those ways of dying that may create particularly sensitive issues for the funeral. Finally, the chapter will think through the specifically Christian dimension of funerals and see how and where the Christian rites are located.

The history of death rites

Douglas Davies in his masterful study *Death, Ritual and Belief* [1] explains that probably the first form of 'funeral' was the act of burying a person in the floor of a cave. Indeed there is archaeological evidence of this going right back to the early Stone Age (some 30,000 years ago). The idea of marking the point of burial of a deceased person also has a significant history. In Malta, for example, there are 2,000-year-old stone structures that probably represent a memorial to the deceased. There is also considerable evidence that earlier forms of funeral rites had a dual role, first to disentangle the life of the person who had died from this world and second to establish the person in the life to come. This remains a feature of the Greek Orthodox ritual. Here the first stage is the burial of the body, where it is left for several years to decay. The second stage is the removal of the skeleton to an ossuary (a special building for the holding of bones).

While burial is probably the oldest form of funeral, the practice of burning the body (or cremation) also has a venerable history. It almost certainly can be traced back to Ancient Greece (evidence for the practice has been found from 2,000 years ago). In addition, there are well-documented examples of cremation being the practice for warriors who died in war. Cremation is, after all, a much easier way of returning the remains of a dead soldier back to the town or village from which he (and in almost all cases it was a 'he') came.

Along with burial with a marked headstone and cremation, there were other forms of dealing with a dead body. Perhaps the most famous example of an alternative is the Lindow Man who was probably a highly respected Briton who died during the period of the Druids 1,800 years ago. He was placed in a peat bog, which, as it happened, preserved his body so effectively that one can see precisely how he died.

The fact that marking the disposal of mortal remains has such a long history should not surprise us. It is undoubtedly a very significant moment. Each type of funeral has a different set of symbols and expectations (some of which we shall look at later in this book). Most aspects of the modern funeral have roots back into antiquity. However, one exception is the modern practice of the funeral home, in which the undertaker transforms and prepares the body. Up until the middle of the nineteenth century, the family handled the arrangements concerning the body after death. The whole concept of an 'undertaker' was of one who undertakes to handle the arrangements. The participation of undertakers (who are increasingly known as funeral directors) is now a feature of the modern funeral and the service provided can be extremely helpful for those who are having to cope with a death.

The growing popularity of cremation

Later in this book we will look at the arguments for and against cremation and burial. At this point it is important simply to document the growing popularity of cremation and some of the reasons for this.

In the UK, cremation is now the most popular form of funeral. In 1992 69 per cent of funerals were cremations. This is extremely high when compared with other countries. In the same year only 19 per cent of funerals in the USA were cremations. The widespread popularity of cremations in the UK has happened relatively quickly; in 1885 only three people were cremated and even in the 1930s only 1 per cent of funerals were cremations. However by 1958 almost a third of all funerals were cremations and a further nine years later the figure had reached 50 per cent. Naturally this growing popularity of cremations required more crematoria. In 1950 there were 58; in 1960, 148; and by 1993 there were 226.[2]

In the UK it is common for even funeral services in church to be followed by a brief service of committal at the crematorium. Unlike in other European countries, the actual burning of the body takes place out of sight of the mourners. Following cremation the next of kin of the deceased have to decide what they want to happen to the ashes. For some it is simply left to the crematorium to place them in the 'Garden of Remembrance'. Others may ask for the ashes to be returned and they are then free to distribute them how they wish. 'Disposal' of ashes may include placing them under a tree in the garden, having them scattered over the sea or perhaps taken to a favourite place of the person who died.

There are a number of reasons for the growth in popularity of cremation. First, it is seen as more 'eco-friendly'. Burial of a body requires more space than that of ashes. Second, many mourners are attracted by the possibility of having the ashes to do with what they will. It creates some attractive possibilities and perhaps may mean that the remains of the person who has just died can be blended into the environment in a host of different ways (whether it be in a meadow, a wood or the ocean). Third, for some it is felt that it helps with the healing process for those who are grieving as there will not necessarily be a grave, which some might feel obliged to visit.

The debates over what to do with remains of a person have been the subject of diplomatic incidents! In the 1950s the Chinese, appalled at the Russian treatment of the hero of the Russian Revolution, Lenin, insisted that in future all senior Chinese officials must be cremated. Lenin had been embalmed and his body was placed on public display in a special mausoleum in Red Square. The Chinese felt that something akin to a cult had developed around Lenin and his tomb. However, as other Communist leaders chose in Hungary, bodies of leaders can always be cremated and the ashes then preserved in a vast, purpose-built building. The ashes of Mahatma Gandhi caused a political crisis in India when, in 1996, some were found in a bank vault in Orissa. Although some of his ashes had been sent to various sacred rivers in India, the rest had simply been stored away. The problem was finally resolved with the decision of the Indian Government to have the remaining ashes placed in the River Ganges.

Going global

All practices in human life arise from a certain context with a certain significance. One can learn a great deal from the exercise of comparison and contrast. Often it is only in seeing how a 'different' culture handles an issue that one appreciates the symbolism and purpose of one's own culture. For example, a person who has been brought up a Roman Catholic may find a visit to a Quaker meeting with its simplicity and silence a very quick way of appreciating the purpose and symbolism of their own Roman Catholic liturgy. Travel, either physical or imaginary, does indeed broaden the mind.

Let us now take an imaginary journey starting in China. China is especially interesting because ancestors have a major and significant place in the extraordinary mix that makes up Chinese religion. Here one will find three stages. The first is the burial. Given this is the least important of the three stages, the place of burial does not matter a great deal. The purpose of this stage is to wait for the body to decompose. The second stage then is to take the bones of the person and intern them into an appropriate container. This container or urn might be reburied to await the third stage, when the container is placed into a permanent tomb.

At the second stage, the person's name is added to the ancestral list. This might be simply a list kept at home or sometimes it will be a list kept in an ancestor hall. The entire rite is organized around the symbolism of the 'ancestor'. For this culture, one's sense of belonging is not just immediate (i.e. the mother and father or sister and brother) but is also firmly located in the wider context of the past and the future. Chinese culture has a strong sense of one's immediate family including all those who have gone before, not just those who are around us here and now. Much of the religious year in China is organized around the symbolism of 'respect' to the ancestors. They are a continuing part of the lives of the living.

Now let us take a second journey, this time to the city of Benares on the River Ganges. What will we find there? Douglas Davies provides a summary:

> The basic pattern of the death ritual is, at one level, quite simple. Dying persons should be laid on the ground with prayers chanted to help them focus on the name of God as they die. After death, the body is washed, dressed and carried home for cremation. During the cremation the skull is cracked by the eldest surviving son . . . after the cremation the remains are thrown into the river.[3]

This simple procedure is rich in symbolism. In Hindu mythology a person is a combination of flesh, which comes from the menstrual flow of the mother, and bones, which come from the semen of the father. As a baby grows in the womb, so it is believed that the 'heat' of the mother enables that growth. After five months of growth in the womb, the life force enters the baby through its head. Douglas explains how the rituals surrounding death mirror this birth process:

> Death, symbolically speaking, parallels this pattern of birth for just as the maternal heat helps produce the foetus so the heat of the cremation fire destroys the flesh, leaving the bones behind. It is as though the elements derived from the female are destroyed, along with the sin of the individual, which is symbolically associated with body hair, itself also destroyed by fire. The remaining bones are placed in the river which is associated with the female principle of existence and thereby, in a symbolic sense, becomes a fertilizing agent . . . [J]ust as the spirit comes to the baby in the womb through its skull so now it departs, through the skull, as the skull is cracked during cremation.[4]

The ritual surrounding death is a mirror of the process of birth. As life has been received in the cycle of birth and rebirth, so this life ends and is passed on to be reborn.

Although we have focused on the rich Hindu symbolism of birth and death, India is probably better known, in ritual terms, for the practice of *sati*. This occurs when the grieving widow decides to join her husband on the funeral pyre and is thus cremated with him. There is considerable argument among scholars whether this practice really is encouraged in the religious tradition. In the Hindu scriptures the *Rig Veda* there is a rite where the woman is described as lying next to her dead husband but then leaves the pyre to go to his living brother. Elsewhere there is a passage that promises great 'glory' for a woman who undergoes this practice.

Numerous rulers and many religious Hindu leaders have opposed the practice of *sati*. It is a custom now completely illegal in modern India, although there are reports that it still occasionally takes place. It should be stressed that such practice was fairly rare and today almost everyone thinks that such 'suicide' is entirely inappropriate.

Before we consider suicide in more detail, it is worth pausing and considering what we can learn from our imaginary journey. From China, we can see the importance of the 'family tree'. In the UK today there are tens of thousands of people who spend significant parts of their free time locating themselves and their children in the context of their own family tree. There are computer programs and websites specially dedicated to helping these genealogists in their task. Others spend their time visiting cemeteries and looking at church records in an attempt to find out what happened to some distant ancestor. It might be that locating ourselves in such a family context is an aspect that we ought to take into account when thinking about planning the details of funerals.

From India, we can see the importance of considering together birth and death. The rituals of death and dying feed the obvious observation that as babies are born so other human beings at the very same moment are dying. Hinduism can teach us that it is entirely right to see that birth and death in this life go hand in hand. There is a natural rhythm to birth, death and new life.

Suicide and euthanasia

The Indian practice of *sati* raised an issue that obviously needs some treatment in a book entitled *The Funeral Handbook*. Suicide can take many different forms. At its most dramatic, it can involve a 'suicide bomber' who is willing to sacrifice his (or occasionally her) life to end the lives of his perceived enemy or to make a political point. More often, suicide is the act of individual persons, acting alone, to curtail their own life. The reasons for such cases can be many, ranging from a strong sense of anger to a sense of hopelessness and despair.

The Christian tradition has largely felt that suicide is wrong, as it is not the same as self-sacrifice. Self-sacrifice occurs when one's prime motive is not to seek death, but to save others and in doing so one sacrifices one's own life. Scott of the Antarctic's companion Lawrence Oates famously left his tent, explaining as he did so that he 'might be gone some time', to free up supplies for his fellow travellers. The reason why suicide generally is wrong is because life is a precious and privileged gift. It is a blessed privilege to have life. Granted, life does have its dark sides, but the expectation and hope of Christianity is that life will be rich in its range of experiences. The gift of life is not something that anyone chooses or earns, it is simply that, a 'gift', granted by the mysterious processes of being. For those who are feeling suicidal, a Christian hope is to work with others to find healing where desperate situations can be converted to hopeful ones.

Voluntary euthanasia is a form of legalized suicide. There is only one country in the world – the Netherlands – that has legalized euthanasia. The conditions for granting a request for euthanasia there are very strict. They require that the patient must have a terminal illness, that the patient must have made repeated requests for euthanasia and the authorities and relatives must have been informed.

Most Christians are opposed to the legalization of euthanasia. In the UK, most doctors do not want to become people who terminate life. Their training and practice is directed towards the saving of lives, not the taking of them. The majority of doctors feel that the legal power to assist in euthanasia might send potentially mixed messages to patients. Most people, they believe, want to know that their doctors are in the business of making people better, not killing them. In addition, there is some concern that it is difficult to be sure the decision made by the patient is not coerced. Many elderly people go through phases of feeling that they are useless or a burden and a drain on the resources of their children and family. To live in a culture where an unscrupulous child, eager for the inheritance, could apply pressure to an old person to sign up for euthanasia would be undesirable.

However, the strongest argument against euthanasia is the dramatic progress in palliative care, which stops attempting to cure the patient, but instead concentrates on ameliorating the symptoms. In other words, terminally ill patients get to the point where they are clear that that they will not recover. They will then be offered palliative care, which in the UK will be in a hospice, a day centre or at home. Palliative care is primarily pain management. One of the remarkable features of the modern day is that pain can be managed so effectively that the vast majority can expect to have, at least physically, a pain-free death. As life approaches the very end, it is not uncommon for a physician to recommend dosages of medication that will ultimately terminate the life of the patient. However, it is important to note that this is not necessarily hastening death. Pain management not only calms the patient, but it can extend life, even when the dosages are very high.

For this reason, in the UK, there is virtual agreement between the medical and nursing professions and religious leaders concerning the value and importance of palliative care. It is felt that to introduce a Voluntary Euthanasia Bill to Parliament or to raise the possibility of such acts being sanctioned through the law courts is unpalatable.

Concluding Christian reflections

As we have seen, the need to mark the occasion of death has a long history and is found in a host of different cultures. The vast majority of cultures do not see death as the end, but rather see it as either a way for the soul to return in a new and different body or as a doorway into a different mode of being.

In the next chapter we will look at the Christian account of what this alternative way of being might be like. However, at the end of this chapter, we need to locate the speculation of the next chapter in the more important framework about what Christians want to claim for this life.

It is wrong to imagine that Christianity is primarily a set of beliefs about the life to come. It is not. It is first and foremost a way of living here and now. The Christian tradition has taught that the great privilege of life (the privilege of breathing and existing moment to moment) is not an accident, but intended. Although human life evolved from simpler forms of life, we need not necessarily assume that the whole process is simply a cosmic accident. Instead, Christians may believe that at the heart of the universe is goodness and love (this is primarily what Christians mean by the word 'God'). It is in the nature of love that it wants to create more 'loving possibilities' and these possibilities are one of the reasons why people may choose to have babies. Here, a couple love each other so much that they may want to express their love for each other by creating another person who can supplement and enhance that love. In the Christian drama God then creates new life. God has, by using the processes of evolution, allowed sentient and complex creatures such as humankind to emerge. As humans, our purpose in being is to discover love and to express love. It is in this process of discovering love that we create things in our lives that Christians believe will last forever.

A Christian hope, therefore, of life beyond the grave should not be viewed as making this life less important. This life matters, because life here and now matters ultimately. Human life becomes more significant because we are called to account for the love we discover and generate as well as for, conversely, the selfishness and hatred we cause. Some people imagine that belief in life after death is partly responsible for the damage that human beings can cause in this world. In this way Richard Dawkins, the biologist teaching at Oxford University, complained after the World Trade Center terrorism that:

> If death is final, a rational agent can be expected to value his life highly and be reluctant to risk it. This makes the world a safer place, just as a plane is safer if its hijacker wants to survive. At the other extreme, if a significant number of people convince themselves, or are convinced by their priests, that a martyr's death is equivalent to pressing the hyperspace button and zooming through a wormhole to another universe, it can make the world a very dangerous place.[5]

Dawkins is right to draw attention to the dark potential of religion. The Christian hope must never be used as an incentive to inflict pain and hurt on others. The Christian story (and, incidentally, the Islamic one) insists that the slaughter of the innocent is a blasphemy against God. However, Dawkins is wrong to imagine that atheists are never going to commit suicide or opt for a misguided set of ideals that require self-sacrifice. Plenty of atheists died for an atheist ideology called Communism. The truth is that both atheists and religious people need to recognize the value of this life and the importance of building up loving relationships within it.

The life of Jesus points to the priority of love. The focus of a Christian funeral, therefore, should very much be the celebration of the life lived. From the very young (who often give much more than is appreciated) to those who have lived a long life (with significant achievements realized), there should be a celebration of the gift and triumph of that life. The Christian hope is that in most lives there is material that God can use to build the person in eternity. This is the belief in 'life after death'. In the next chapter we shall speculate a little on whether this belief makes sense in the modern world. Whether it does or does not, it is important to stress that it is not essential to the Christian understanding of either the funeral or the importance of this life. A funeral marks an important moment even if there is nothing beyond. There are plenty of good reasons to mark the end of life with ritual even if death is the end of that individual person. The gift of life had been granted, a life had been lived and a life has now ended. These facts in themselves are enough to demonstrate why the end of human life should be marked.

CHAPTER THREE

Christianity and Death

Given that death is universal, it is not surprising that there are many different explanations about what exactly happens at death. We all agree that biologically the heart stops beating and mental activity ceases, but beyond that there is considerable disagreement. Indeed historically and geographically, we find a vast array of different accounts of death. In India, for instance, reincarnation is the dominant view. This view believes that death is simply a bridge where the soul leaves one person to become reincarnated into another person's body. For Christians and Muslims, however, the traditional view has been that each unique soul will find itself either in heaven or hell.

In Europe today, there is a widespread view that death is the end. Indeed some thinkers believe that this is not only scientifically more plausible, but also ethically superior. The advantage of insisting that 'this life is it' is that it means that one will focus all the more effectively on this life. Indeed Karl Marx's great complaint about life after death is that it became for the poor and oppressed the great hope that was supposed to help them cope with the injustices of this life. Marx wanted the poor to stop hoping for life beyond the grave and start sorting life out here and now. Religion, he said, was the opium of the people.

All Christians would concede that it is wrong for a guarantee of life beyond the grave to become an excuse for not changing life here and now. For some Christians there is a sense that Christianity should be more focused on life here and now and less worried about life after death. Such Christians would point to the way in which the expression 'eternal life' is used in John's Gospel. There, eternal life is not seen as a state in heaven, but a quality of life that starts now. This Johannine view is that to be faithful to God in this life is to discover those supreme values that God represents and to live them as fully as possible.

However, for other Christians, the sense that this life is part of a bigger picture is important. The fact that this life is a significant part of a greater whole gives this earthly life its value. Love matters simply because it matters eternally. Ultimately *people* matter simply because they are created to partake in the life of God for eternity. Immortality matters because it becomes the context in which we determine what ultimately concerns us.

For most Christians, the main reason why they believe in some survival beyond the grave is the resurrection of Jesus. St Paul claimed that 'if Christ has not been raised, then our proclamation has been in vain and your faith has been in vain' (1 Corinthians 15.14). The Jesus movement developed because those around him believed that he had conquered death.

Furthermore, the most significant reason why most Christians are committed to believing that we live on beyond death is that it is an important part of the explanation as to how and why evil and suffering are permitted. If there was not a bigger picture, then most explanations sound very feeble in the light of so much suffering. 'Suffering is good for character' works only in a limited way. It becomes obscene when issues such as rape, child abuse or the Jewish Holocaust are confronted. Too often in such situations character is destroyed. In short, those values that are only possible through suffering become cruelly absurd when death takes the sufferer to oblivion. This is not to say that some 'pie in the sky' somehow justifies suffering, but rather that the ways in which values are discovered through suffering have an eternal significance. This is not compensation because there is an organic connection between suffering and its results in the individual's life, and the fruition of those results in eternity. This helps provide a perspective for suffering that enables us to see that the values emerging from suffering do have a preciousness.

For many people this sense of hope that can make sense of

human suffering is sufficient and they do not feel the need to wrestle with the details about how it is possible. However, for others, perhaps those with a more scientific mindset, it is important to think through how these things can be possible. What follows in the next part of this chapter is for those who find this way of thinking interesting. If such issues hold little interest for you, however, please feel free to skip the next section and move on to the end of the chapter.

What it means to be human

For Christians, one fundamental idea of their faith is that all humans are created in the image of God. This sounds straight-forward but what exactly does it mean? Does it mean that we are different from all the (non-human) animals? For some critics of Christianity, this is a very problematic doctrine. They ask, why should humans think they are so special? Two groups in particular have raised certain difficulties with the idea that humans are made in the image of God.

The first group is the 'deep ecology' group. Shallow ecology is where one is worried about the environment because of a concern to make sure that humans still have a planet to enjoy. Deep ecology is committed to the planet because the planet itself has intrinsic value, independent of its value to humans. Value, for deep ecologists, is not imposed from outside – from the human perspective – rather, each part of the environment has its own place and role and is acknowledged to be equally as significant and equally as precious as the rest. From this point of view, it is a human conceit to claim that humans are more significant than hedgehogs or mountains. It is not only conceited, deep ecologists argue, but deeply damaging. Under the banner of such state-ments as 'humans are the only things that matter', humans use and destroy animals, plants and geology.

We can and should affirm the concern that underpins deep

ecology, but we also do want to affirm the doctrine that people are made in God's image. To insist that everything is equally significant rapidly becomes a non-sense. A carrot is important, but morally it is correctly seen as less important than a dog. Dogs have feelings and capacities for relationships that carrots do not. It is the complexity of a dog that entitles it to more rights and greater care. For all the reasons that dogs exceed carrots, so humans exceed dogs. This is a point we will return to in a moment.

There is a second objection that needs to be discussed. It comes from the Australian philosopher Peter Singer. Singer has coined the expression 'speciesism' to describe the vice of valuing one species over others for no good reason. The reasons that people normally cite for preferring humans to other living things are the intelligence, moral awareness, language and capacity for thought that humans possess. Not all humans, however, have all these attributes. Babies, the severely mentally ill and the very old may not have the same power of speech or as much intelligence as other human beings. Non-human animals (especially the higher primates) have much better 'speech' and powers of reasoning than human babies. We do not, however, exclude babies and include gorillas in our preferences because of this. Such choices, Peter Singer says, expose the affirmation of the human as a prejudice: Christians are guilty of speciesism.

Singer is right to insist that some of the important characteristics of the human species are found outside the human community. Dolphins are highly intelligent, for instance; and the higher primates can, in some respects, mirror human communities (admittedly to a lesser degree). This leads us to believe that there is a sliding scale of rights. According to this scale humans are more significant than any other form of life but gorillas and dolphins are more significant than say mice, while mice are more significant than daisies. Other animals and plants should be judged against these same criteria.

Singer, however, is wrong to insist that a definition of a species should encompass the less developed and mal-developed. To do that would be like defining an eye with respect to blindness, simply because for some people, tragically, their eyes do not operate properly. Babies have a potential that a gorilla does not. Those elderly humans who deteriorate so much that speech becomes impossible or those who are born with severe Down's syndrome are, in part, analogous to those who are asleep. Keith Ward, the English theologian, makes the point well, when he writes:

> Just as a person who is asleep does not use his or her rational powers, so a mentally handicapped person is prevented from using such powers, often throughout a whole lifetime. The subject of their consciousness is not non-human, or that proper to an animal. It is human, belonging to the human species, but is deprived of its proper form of activity.[1]

Humanity should be defined by the characteristics true of humans in their normal mode; that is, developed, awake and well. When we are less developed or asleep or ill we are still human, even if we are unable to use and enjoy all the capacities and gifts of being human.

It is important to defend the idea that people are made in God's image. It explains why it is so evil to take an indifferent attitude to human life as did, for instance, those responsible for concentration camps during the Second World War. It is also important for all those concerned with ecology. The idea of humans being made in the image of God projects human responsibility. We have been created with the capacity to use our power for good or ill. This is what 'God's image' means. The privilege of being human involves responsibility. If humans have no greater value (and therefore no greater rights and responsibilities) than any other part of the environment, then to criticize and exhort humans to behave more responsibly becomes a non-sense. For the ecological crisis to be tackled, we need to persuade more people that we have the power to adjust our priorities and act justly towards the environment.

So far, we have defended the idea of the image of God from objections. But what else ought we to say about it? The doctrine has its roots in the famous opening chapter of the Bible, which reads:

> Then God said, 'Let us make humankind in our image, according to our likeness; and let them have dominion over the fish of the sea, and over the birds of the air, and over the cattle, and over all the wild animals of the earth, and over every creeping thing that creeps upon the earth.' So God created humankind in his image. (Genesis 1.26–7)

The point of this passage is that humans share in a special way something of the creative power and responsibilities of the Creator. What exactly, however, does this mean? Among the early Church Fathers (leaders who formulated much of Christian doctrine in the early centuries of the Church), there was a difference of emphasis. Augustine stressed human reason, which reflected the wisdom of God, while Athanasius emphasized humankind's unique potential for relationship with God. Both of these strands are important and should be linked together. Human reason and our capacity for relationships depend on

- the capacity for language, which is the distinctive gift of reason,
- the capacity for love and intimacy, supremely with God,
- the gift of freedom, and
- our moral awareness.

Language marks out the human species. Clearly other animals

have a limited range of signals and noises that provide basic forms of communication, but human language is unique in its effectiveness. Experience is organized, evaluated and controlled through language. It is a precondition for all other human activities. Relationships that transcend the instinctive – that warrant the language of love – are also a marked feature of human communities. We can give ourselves to others and share each other's lives. This is true not only on the human level, but also on the divine. Freedom is a prerequisite of love. One cannot love if one is compelled. To use an analogy, it is very easy to set up one's computer with a loving message on the screen saver, but the message lacks profound significance precisely because it has been programmed. One does not value a declaration of love from a machine. The capacity to choose and take responsibility for choice is an important element of being human. Love is the expression of freedom.

Moral capacity is implied in the above, yet it stands alone in embracing all those defining decisions that determine our openness to love or self. Language, our capacity for relationships, freedom, and moral discernment are all the defining characteristics of being human. They are thus the reasons why it is a privilege to be human. This then is earthly human life, made in the image of God, but what happens after we die?

Living for eternity

Of course, no one knows for sure what life beyond the grave is going to be like. We are at this point forced to resort to 'revelation' (i.e. some source that religious people believe has authority because it reveals God to us). Different religious traditions have given different accounts of what this divine revelation consists of. If one asked a Hindu, for example, she would give a different answer from that of a Christian. Furthermore, different types of Hindu or different types of Christian will give different answers while speaking from the same religious traditions. It is important to appreciate that there is no uniform, universal, Christian position. It is, however, worth noting at this point that the answers given by different religious traditions are not completely different. Most traditions stress some element of judgement (that we must take responsibility for the decisions made in this life). Most also aspire to some state of harmony, where love and freedom finally coincide (where the radical flaws in earthly life are absent). However, even with these broad areas of agreement, there are significant differences. What follows is one picture of what 'eternal life' means. It is one that we believe makes sense but it is also one with which others will disagree.

As Christians we turn to the resources of our tradition. Life after death is relatively unimportant in the Hebrew Bible (the Old Testament). In the texts that make up this part of the Bible, God's judgement of the nations tends to occur in this world alone. The Christian Scriptures, however (the New Testament), were written when expectations of the end of the world, coupled with a general resurrection, were widespread. Such beliefs became central themes within the New Testament since they were all written in the light of the experience of the resurrection of Jesus.

The precise nature of the historical event underpinning the story that was told after Jesus' death, that 'he is alive', is now unobtainable to us. We cannot get behind the differing descriptions found in the first letter to the Corinthians and in the Gospels according to Matthew, Mark, Luke and John. All the authors of these texts agree that the experience is 'real' and life-transforming. They also take the resurrection of Jesus to be a model of the general resurrection to come. From this, perhaps we can work out the following.

On the whole, the Christian tradition has been committed to a view of humanity as what some philosophers have called a 'psychosomatic unity'. This rather complicated technical terminology simply means that people are made up of an integrated unity, consisting of body and soul. The view that the body is useless but that the 'soul' of the person is what alone survives death is not the dominant view of the Church. Philosophically, this picture of a disembodied soul is difficult to understand. For most Christians, when they imagine life beyond the grave, they imagine a state in which humans have a mental life (i.e. thoughts, etc.) located within a body. This is what St Paul saw as a transformed self. The precise nature of the body is difficult to describe. Just as there is a different flesh for animals and humans, so there will be different bodies for life on earth and life in heaven (see 1 Corinthians 15.39). It seems reasonable that human life after death may consist of individuals having bodies that will operate significantly differently from their present ones. Presumably such a state would need some different sort of space/time framework (it is difficult to see how bodies could be without such), in which we will not be subject to the bodily restrictions that we currently endure.

This brief sketch is grounded in the New Testament talk about resurrection. Philosophically there is a significant, big problem with life beyond the grave because of the death gap. This death gap makes 'certain identification' very difficult. How do we know that the person who earlier today drank a cup of coffee is the same person who is reading this chapter now? One very good answer is that there has been bodily continuity. In other words, the bundle of atoms that comprise 'you' continues to exist in space and time from since you had your earlier cup of coffee to reading this page now. Some philosophers, however, find it difficult to imagine personal identity overcoming these gaps in bodily continuity.

In order to help answer this problem let us imagine a thought exercise (one that is adapted from the contemporary English philosopher, Keith Ward). Suppose that all children, at the age of eight, suddenly disappear for two minutes and then reappear as humanoid-birds. The process undergone is much like a caterpillar changing into a butterfly, but with a short gap to enable the transformation to take place. Now, while this sounds odd to us, if it were universal it would appear completely normal. The humanoid-bird would share many of the characteristics of the child. It would remember being a child. It would have the same basic character and personality as the child. However, once it became a humanoid-bird, its character would inevitably change, in much the same way as the character of a person who recovers the ability to walk after being confined to a wheelchair for ten years changes. The point being made by Ward here is simple. If this were merely a part of the natural process, we would rapidly become accustomed to talking about the humanoid-bird as identical to the child. If the process went wrong, which from time to time it probably would, and two humanoid-birds emerged, then we would probably talk about the child splitting into two birds and require that each should be treated as an autonomous individual.

Keith Ward suggests that life beyond the grave will be a similar change to the above. He suggests that we are similar to the children who will become transformed into humanoid-birds. After death our characters will transfer from our existing bodies into their heavenly bodies. These heavenly bodies will enable different possibilities to take place that will bring about change and development in our characters. Ward feels that it is important to build on our character similarities and yet to embrace them within certain differences.

This picture has been loosely built on the resurrection of Jesus. Many Christians think it can make sense to imagine a resurrection, with a mind in a body, operating in a space/time framework, in which individuals will be recognizable. However, thus far in this chapter we have just considered eternal life involving humankind, but what about the rest of creation?

A redeemed creation

When seen from the view of some Christians, the doctrine of the creation of the world seems more attractive than that of the redemption of the world at the end of time. Creation consists of the whole of the cosmic order (with the earth as one small part of it). It is rich in its diversity and beauty. In contrast, however, for these same Christians, redemption at the end of time is simply confined to humankind alone and then only a very small part of that. Such Christians insist that Muslims or Buddhists or even some branches of the Christian family will not be saved at the end of time. In questioning such a view the writers of this book cannot help but wonder why God bothered with animals and plants and the rest of creation if the end result involves their exclusion. Surely we should expect the scale of redemption to be at least equivalent to that of creation?

In the letter to the Romans in the New Testament, St Paul insists that the 'creation itself will be set free from its bondage to decay and will obtain the freedom of the glory of the children of God' (Romans 8.21). The book of Revelation talks about a 'new heaven and a new earth' (Revelation 21.1). In addition to the more narrow view of redemption in the paragraph above, there is a strong strand in the Christian tradition that holds that all of creation will ultimately be redeemed. We think this strand should be taken seriously.

While admitting that all talk concerning the end of time and what happens after death is speculative, it does seem reasonable to believe that in some way, analogous to the normal developing and changing of a human life in the here and now, all matter and life will be transformed at the end of time. One of the great theologians of the twentieth century, Jürgen Moltmann brought the significance of Jesus' resurrection together with a cosmic view that justified the redemption of the entire creation. He wrote:

> If the day of Christ's resurrection is the first day of the new creation, then it also brings the creation of new light, a light

which lights up not merely sense but the mind and spirit too, and shines over the whole new creation . . . In the Epistle to the Colossians a vision of cosmic peace is developed which is grounded on *a cosmic christology*. Through Christ everything will be reconciled 'whether on earth or in heaven, making peace by the blood of his cross, through himself (1.20) . . . He [Christ] died . . . so as to reconcile everything in heaven and on earth, which means the angels and the beasts too, and to bring peace to the whole creation . . . If Christ has died not merely for the reconciliation of human beings, but for the reconciliation of all other creatures too, then every created being enjoys infinite value in God's sight, and has its own right to live; this is not true of human beings alone.[2]

In short, Moltmann argues, if Jesus died for the whole world, then we should reasonably expect the whole world to be redeemed at the end of time. In some sense, animals, plants and the whole of creation will have a place in the life to come.

Hell

For many as they approach death, it is not the hope of heaven that preoccupies them, but the fear of hell. Hell is the state of unrelenting punishment by God for the wickedness that we have done on earth. For some Christians, hell is believed to be the destination for all those who are not Christians.

Although it is true that we will all have to face up to the consequences of our behaviour on earth, we are not persuaded about such a reality as hell. The problems with such a straightforward doctrine of hell seem overwhelming. To divide humanity into those deserving of heaven and those deserving of hell seems impossible. There are plenty of Christians who thwart love while there are equally plenty of non-believers who exhibit all the 'fruits of the spirit' (love and kindness, etc.) that St Paul talks about. An eternity of punishment seems disproportionate for a lifetime of wickedness, even if one has been exceptionally wicked. Beside this, the Christian good news (the gospel) is about Christ dying for the whole world so that the whole world is redeemed.

In our view, hell as traditionally described is very unlikely. Instead we, like many Christians, see hell as a state of 'selfishness' and 'loneliness' that we create for ourselves. Hell is very much a state of mind that we can and do create here on earth. As we discover love, so we discover the life of God, and as we create barriers of hatred, so we create hell. It is possible that when we die some of us, perhaps most of us, will still have barriers that will need destroying. This is the problematic area that the doctrine of purgatory set out to resolve. It would be wrong to get too mathematical and attempt to calculate precisely the time in purgatory that each sin is likely to accrue. Instead it is our view that human barriers created by individuals need to be destroyed by love, and that this process should start in this life and might require some time in the life to come to bring it to completion.

All this and the funeral

These reflections and speculations set the scene in which the funeral takes place, although at the time they may seem peripheral to the process of organizing the funeral. By the time the funeral comes about the destination of that person's essence is simply in the 'hands of God'. At such time we simply trust that the Creator of the universe will do right. We do not need to, and nor should we, speculate about the likely nature of life beyond the grave.

Yet we have included our analysis (and we stress that it is simply our view – there are plenty of alternative accounts) because we do believe that the funeral should be viewed as a positive occasion. It is, if you like, the doorway to transformation. As we will see later in the book, as well as being a time for sorrow the funeral ought to be a celebration of the life lived and an occasion for great hope. The hope will be that all the problems that make up a human life are caught up in the drama of God's redemption and transformed into building blocks for the occasion of love.

The Christian hope is important. We need constantly to retain the sense that our life is a small part of a greater whole. It is only from this perspective that much that appears difficult and odd now will ultimately be seen to form a pattern that can be used by God for eternity.

CHAPTER FOUR

Attitudes towards Death

Thinking about dying and death can be difficult, because our Western culture has removed death from the agenda of much of life. Where once our forebears lived with death around them each week, today most deaths take place in hospitals and our modern attitude could now be characterized as 'out of sight out of mind'. Where once talking of sex was the big taboo, today many shy away from talking about death, while they are now quite happy to talk and read about sex in a way formerly unimaginable. In addition to the reticence of seeing death as natural and unavoidable, many see it as something to be ashamed of or regard death almost as a failure of medical science. When death is talked about in Western society it is often in a way that many skilled in promoting good mental well-being (clergy, counsellors, psychiatrists, for instance) see as being unhealthy and sometimes damaging. Modern Western culture seems to have generated a set of beliefs that are untrue and unhelpful in coming to terms with death and dying. Our task in this chapter is to name these false beliefs and explain precisely why they should be challenged and replaced with something better.

The point of this exercise is to make one very simple and important point. Although Christians are confident of a hope of life that triumphs over death, it is still the case that there is a sense of loss here and now. This is a loss that we will live with until we ourselves die, and is something that we do not need to try to remove from our feelings nor should we be ashamed about it. How we handle that sense of loss will depend on a whole multitude of factors. This loss is highly individual and it is rarely easy to deal with.

False belief one: *it is easier to cope with the death of an old person than the death of a young person*

Even though this is an understandable misconception, it is nevertheless mistaken. It is understandable because there is a sense of horror when death strikes the very young. The death of a child is a crippling tragedy; the sudden loss of potential and the destruction of innocence leaves a deep sense of bewilderment. What is not the case, however, is that because the death of a young person is tragic, then the death of an older person is less terrible and is therefore easier to deal with. Just because someone dies in their eighties or nineties does not necessarily mean that it should be more easily handled.

When someone dies in their eighties or nineties, there is a lifetime of patterns that have grown up around that person. Indeed, the sense that a parent will always be around and part of your life has been generated. For decades (perhaps eight or nine decades) that person has been a significant part of your life and the connections with her or him have become part of your own identity. It is easy to take for granted that just as the universe has a sun, a moon, planets and stars, and will have for all of your life, so too your parent (or other loved one) will be around forever in the same way. You don't wake up each morning worrying about the continuing planetary positions, and this same attitude is assumed towards your elderly relative or friend.

It is not, therefore, that a young person's death is trivial, but that the death of both young and old can be deeply traumatic. The observation that 'Fred at least had a good innings' is often unhelpful. This is no compensation for the gap left in the life of those who survived. Acknowledging this gap is an important aspect in the process of accepting the death and moving on with one's own life.

False belief two: *an unexpected death is harder to cope with than one that is the result of a long illness*

This misconception plays to an intuition that, in emotional terms, shock is harder than preparation and that a deep traumatic shock involving the sudden death of a loved one can be very difficult. A death resulting from a car accident or sudden heart attack, where the person dies almost instantaneously, provides no opportunity for the final goodbye, a last cuddle or squeeze of the hand. In living busy lives, it is easy to start the working day without demonstrating the underlying love we feel for those close to us. In such circumstances the unexpected death seems so harsh and capricious that it looks as if it is bound to be harder to cope with than the one where there have been days, months or even years of preparation.

However, what such an attitude overlooks is that sustained periods of illness also bring their own stresses and demands. Watching the gradual deterioration of a loved one can be a heart-wrenching obligation. Illness can distort the personality. In illnesses parts of personality such as a great sense of humour may disappear behind the person's daily struggles to cope with the pain she feels. Perhaps the lively mind that has engaged the world with great vitality becomes muddled and confused. Living with illness can be extremely difficult for both those who are suffering and for those who are watching and caring.

In addition to the anguish that often comes with waiting alongside those who are suffering comes the feeling of hope. The thought that this current period of illness affords numerous opportunities for a sense of preparedness for death to emerge can disappear underneath a perhaps unrealistic hope that this stage will pass and recovery is imminent. New medical technologies will be tried; prayer and other hopes to bring about recovery will be invoked. All this can lead to the further strain of endless false dawns and with them accompanying frustration.

Finally, a long, sustained illness can often leave deep scars of guilt. It is not uncommon for both the person dying and those watching to find the language of euthanasia or even the passing thought of suicide a temptation. One might almost feel 'relieved' that death has been the final release from pain. This relief can become a problem because later the bereavement process might have to additionally handle an added sense of guilt, which might make a person wonder how authentic the love they felt really was. Again, the truth is that both the shocking death and the death after a sustained period of illness are difficult to handle. Both bring their distinctive problems, which will need to be confronted and handled with sensitivity.

False belief three: *people find it easier to handle bereavement better when they are older; it is much harder to cope with death when one is younger*

Losing a parent in one's teenage years seems so manifestly tragic that one imagines that it must be easier to cope with the death of a parent when one is aged, say, 60. It is easy to think that the teenager has enjoyed the relationship for only a limited number of years and that, in addition, he lacks the resources that maturity brings to locate and place the tragedy into perspective.

Yet what such an attitude ignores is that maturity is a limited aid for coping with these sad, unique moments in a life. A parent can have a highly individual connection with her child. Maturity is helpful in handling repeated problems in life. For instance, the adolescent romance that fails after a couple of days and then becomes the 'end of the world' for the teenager because it is the first of many moments of unrequited love can be dealt with wholly differently by a person in their thirties. However, the death of a parent is not a 'repeat' problem, which can be learnt to be coped with better each time. Similarly, the death of other relatives or friends is no substitute for the unique way in which each of their particular deaths might touch you. Maturity gives you no preparation for the unique tragedy and gap that a particular death can bring.

False belief four: *you are finally 'over' the death of a loved one when you start to enjoy life again*

This perhaps is the most pernicious false belief of all. It works in a variety of different ways. It is possible for someone to die and for a grieving person to see the funny side to life 24 hours later. This does not mean, however, that the bereaved person is indifferent to the tragedy that has just befallen him. Coping with bereavement is a highly individual process, and the true impact is often perhaps felt only months or years later. Conversely, it is true that for some people the sense of 'shock' and 'numbness' leaves them deeply preoccupied and unable to find it possible to laugh at anything in life for the time being.

The point here is simple; one should always seek to recognize the way that one feels and not try to deny what is felt or to behave in a way that feels unnatural or false. If one is feeling anger, then it is right that this anger is expressed in some way. If one is feeling sad, then a 'good cry' might be precisely what is needed. Also if the bereaved person wants to smile, to laugh or to crack a joke, then he should feel free to do so. It is important not to let the expectations of those around you determine how you should behave (although it is right that you should be sensitive to how any other people around you, who may also be bereaved, may be feeling). In the end each individual bereaved person has to cope with bereavement in their own way and is entitled to find and use whatever reasonable means of coping helps them best.

Later in this book we shall look at the different kinds of funerals that people find help them mourn a death and express what is felt about the deceased person. One of the purposes of this comparative exercise will be to reinforce the simple point that has been made in this chapter, that much of our cultural conditioning (the way that Western culture has shaped our thinking) can be problematic. Some find it helpful to consider also the experiences of other cultures in dealing with death and dying. Doing so can expose us to some of the alternatives and make us think about the appropriateness of our own assumptions. When, later in this book, we look at what alternatives some British people have made towards death rituals, as with all material in this book, do not feel obliged to read it. This book is a handbook, which can be dipped in and out of, and it is not intended as a manual for all people to use in all circumstances. Readers should feel free to skip any section and move onto those that they find more helpful or applicable for their particular circumstances.

CHAPTER FIVE

Financial Matters

In this chapter, our attention will turn once again to focus on the person preparing for her or his own death. The chapter will deal with all of the practical questions that surround the legal document, the will, and those that are concerned with the finances. Before such issues are examined in the greater part of the chapter, however, we begin by pausing and giving some thought to the appropriateness or otherwise of Christians worrying about such monetary matters.

One immediate problem, which might arise for some Christians, is to be found in the Sermon on the Mount, which is a central part of the teaching of Jesus (this is found in Matthew's Gospel, chapters 5 to 7). Here Jesus taught, 'Do not worry about tomorrow, for tomorrow will bring worries of its own. Today's trouble is enough for today' (Matthew 6.34). He also said, 'Look at the birds of the air; they neither sow nor reap nor gather into barns, and yet your heavenly Father feeds them. Are you not of more value than they?' (Matthew 6.26). What Jesus is stressing in these passages is that it is important to keep all these practical arrangements in perspective. Life, Jesus says, is more than worrying about what we will wear or what we will eat or drink.

Every day on the television news or in the newspapers we find examples of devastated lives, where the 'best laid plans of mice and men' do not work. In the end we have to live by trust. We have to trust that the world will remain fundamentally ordered and that it will remain something to have trust in. We should not imagine that we will be able to foresee every possible eventuality of our actions or inaction. There are a million and one things that could happen that we cannot anticipate and cannot protect ourselves or our loved ones from. Every day as we wake, as far as is reasonably possible, it is appropriate that we should be thankful. We should try to be grateful that we find ourselves in a home, when many do not; grateful that the day is relatively predictable, when for many the day is anything but predictable; and we should be grateful that we can be fairly confident that at the end of the day, it is likely we will be climbing back into the same bed. There are many people, both over the centuries and – to what should be the world's shame – today, who have not been able to enjoy such good fortune and privilege.

So with the sense that Christians do their planning tentatively (and gratefully), we can now embark on the exercise of planning with which this chapter is concerned. As in all things in life, big or small, Christians should try to place their efforts of this financial planning within the context of prayer. In deciding how to use your money (whether that is a large or small amount) you are making some important decisions that may affect significantly the lives of those whom you leave behind.

Facing up to the financial implications

Many people have concerns about the financial impact their death will have upon their loved ones. Most also have a good idea of who they wish to receive any money or assets from their estate, be it family, friends or charities. However, for many, knowing how to actually put legal documentation in place to carry out their wishes can seem like a minefield.

There are several aspects to consider:

- Life assurance
- Making a will
- Choosing executors
- Inheritance tax
- Funeral payment

We will consider each of these topics in turn. This book is not intended to advise you on these highly technical areas and we recommend that you should seek advice from an independent financial advisor, a solicitor, an accountant, or all three. The purpose of this chapter, however, is to highlight the areas that you should consider either in preparation of your own affairs or as an executor of a will. It will serve as a good introduction to the subjects to be considered and this will prove to be a useful background for you before you see an independent financial advisor, solicitor or accountant.

Life assurance

Life assurance, also known as life insurance, comes in many shapes and forms and is offered by a large number of companies. It can be complicated deciding which, if any, is best for you but a financial advisor should be able to help in this process.

There are various types of financial advisor. Some are attached to a particular company and will offer only the products that their company provides; other advisors will offer a range of products from a limited number of different companies. An independent financial advisor should be able to advise you on any product on the market suitable for you. They are not linked to any specific companies. You should check which sort of financial advisor you are receiving advice from and decide which offers the best for your needs. The majority of financial advisors are paid by taking a percentage of the premiums that you pay; this is called their commission. This is often convenient because you do not have to pay for their fees 'up front'. However, you should ask how much their commission is, since it may vary from company to company. Some advisors will charge a fee rather than commission, which may prove cheaper in some instances.

Whether you need life assurance will probably be dependent upon your age and the size of your debts, if any. The most likely candidates are those with mortgages and/or children of school age and younger. Life assurance, depending upon the amount insured, might be used to pay off the mortgage and leave an amount for any dependent spouse, partner or children to live on. A retired couple who have fully paid their mortgage may be less likely to require a substantial amount of life assurance. However, even in this case, a surviving spouse will still need sufficient income to pay for funeral expenses and continue a similar lifestyle without the need to sell the house for income.

Where a substantial inheritance might be left, some people take out life assurance to pay for any inheritance tax bill so that the estate remains intact for their dependents.

Making a will

Most people discuss with others their wishes for the distribution of their estate. 'Estate' means the total amount of money and assets a person leaves upon their death. It is, however, vital that these wishes are contained within a legal document for them to be effected in the event of a person's death. This legal document is a will and it must be witnessed and kept in a safe place. You must ensure that your executors know where the will is kept and possibly you should even give them a copy. You should also consider revisiting your will every few years to ensure that it still reflects your wishes. It may be that further children or grand-children have been born or that other beneficiaries have died since you last revised your will.

If you die without a will, you die 'intestate'. Your estate will then be distributed according to the laws of intestacy, which may not reflect your wishes. The law tries to provide for your family first but it will not automatically take into account an unmarried partner or a friend or favourite charity. Your spouse is entitled to all of your personal possessions such as clothes, books, furniture and car. Your spouse also inherits the value of the estate up to £125,000 (this figure may change each year, depending on what amount the Chancellor of the Exchequer decides upon).

If there are children, the spouse receives the personal possessions plus £125,000; the remainder of the estate is divided into two. One half goes to the children; the other half is held in trust for the spouse to live off the income; when the spouse dies, the children receive the assets of the trust. This could leave the surviving spouse with less income since a significant proportion of the estate has passed directly to the children. If you die with no spouse or children, the estate will then be distributed to more distant relatives. If no relatives can be traced the estate could ultimately go to the Crown.

Making a will is not difficult if your affairs are relatively straightforward. There are many books, computer software packages and websites that show you how to write your own will. There are also forms that you can buy in stationers' shops to help you. There could be pitfalls in drawing up your own will since it needs to be legally correct so, if in doubt, seek advice from an expert. The alternative is to ask a solicitor to draw one up for you. Ask for a quote before you proceed; the cost should reflect the complexity of your personal circumstances.

It is also important to make a will if you have children of school age or under because you may wish to appoint a guardian who would take care of them if you die without a partner or your partner dies with you. With many children living with step-parents, it is not always clear who should be the guardian if a natural parent dies. This is a difficult topic to raise but it is essential for the children to be considered.

Choosing executors

An executor is the person who will deal with the administration of your will and ensure that your wishes therein are carried out. The executor may need to liaise with a solicitor to ensure that the estate is correctly distributed among the beneficiaries. It is necessary to obtain 'probate', which is the legal process of deciding that someone's will has been properly made and can be carried out. Probate must be obtained before the estate can be distributed. The executor may also need to deal with returns to the Inland Revenue to quantify any inheritance tax payable.

It is common to choose a relative to be the executor of a will. It is possible to have more than one executor and this may be advisable if there will be a lot of work involved. While a relative is often the person who knows best what the will writer's (testator) intentions were, it must be borne in mind that it can be a very stressful time when someone dies and being executor may be too much for some relatives to cope with.

You may wish to consider having your solicitor or accountant as executor, or possibly as a joint executor. This relieves some of the pressure from relatives and is certainly a major consideration if there are likely to be disputes over the will or if there are technical issues to be dealt with. It is likely that a professional executor will charge fees.

Inheritance tax

Inheritance tax (IHT), often referred to as death duties, is not payable on most estates and therefore people generally do not consider it to be an issue for them. IHT is generally paid on an estate that is valued on death at more than £250,000 (this is the April 2002 figure and has generally been increased by a small amount each year by the Chancellor of the Exchequer). This amount is referred to as the nil rate band and can be reached quite easily by people who own their home together with the value of any pension and life assurance. So many more people can be caught in the IHT net than it would originally appear. IHT is payable at 40 per cent (2002/3 rates).

There is no inheritance tax payable on an estate that passes between husband and wife provided both are domiciled in the UK. The law surrounding domicile can be complicated and you should consult an expert if either husband or wife was born outside of the UK or intends to reside permanently outside the UK.

Inheritance tax is not just a tax at death. It is in fact a tax on transferring value from one person to another; for example, a gift of an asset or cash. So any gifts (transfers) made during someone's lifetime are also potentially subject to IHT. Most, however, are likely to fall under an exemption or relief and not become immediately chargeable to tax. The most common exemption is the potentially exempt transfer (PET), which applies to most lifetime transfers. There is no immediate charge to IHT although the transfers do not actually fall out of charge to IHT until seven years have passed. If the person making the transfer dies before seven years have passed, provided at least three years have passed, there is a sliding scale called taper relief that helps reduce the amount of tax payable.

If it is possible for assets to be given away during your lifetime, you may ultimately reduce the inheritance tax bill of your estate. The only problem is that you must relinquish all rights to the asset and you are unlikely to want to endure hardship in your retirement because you have given all of your hard-earned cash and assets away! You should only gift amounts that you can afford to be without. It is also often the case that your house is your most valuable asset and, at first sight, making yourself homeless is not likely to be a palatable option.

Assets up to £3,000 may be gifted each year free of IHT; this represents the annual exemption. Gifts can also be made on the occasion of marriage up to £5,000, depending upon the relationship between the donor and the recipient (parents may give up to £5,000 tax-free, grandparents £2,500 and others £1,000).

It is also possible to make gifts out of income that will not attract IHT. The amounts must be out of income, not capital, and it may be necessary to prove that the amounts are surplus to the requirements of the donor. It is also beneficial to indicate that there is a sustainable pattern to the gifts to demonstrate that they are genuinely out of income and not one-off transfers of capital. There are special reliefs available for 'business property' and 'agricultural property', which help pass on family and unquoted businesses and farms free of IHT. It is strongly recommended that professional advice be sought under these circumstances to ensure that the relief is applicable and is used to the full where available.

There are certain tax planning schemes that attempt to reduce your IHT liability, many involving trusts. It might be advisable to contact your accountant, solicitor, tax advisor or financial advisor if you think these may be applicable to you. You will undoubtedly be charged for the advice but it could save considerable amounts of IHT and keep your bequests more intact.

We noted above that there is no IHT payable on transfers between husband and wife. However, when the second spouse dies there will be a charge on the whole remaining estate. In effect, the first spouse to die does not utilize their nil rate band. It is therefore advisable to see whether some of the value of the estate up to the nil rate band can be used on the first death; for example, not leaving all assets to the spouse but leaving some to say the children as well. Again this is only advisable if there is sufficient to allow the surviving spouse to live comfortably. There are schemes with trusts that enable the surviving spouse to live off the income of assets although the actual assets are no longer legally hers, and these could be of use in certain situations. Again, proper advice would need to be sought.

Any death benefits payable by a pension fund can usually be written into trust to avoid them being part of the estate subject to IHT on death. You should contact your pension advisor to discuss whether this is relevant in your case since pensions can often amount to a sizeable part of your estate.

Funeral payment

While it is not necessary for a person to think about the payment for their own funeral nevertheless many people do make provision for this so as not to burden their nearest and dearest with extra work or expense. Prepaid funeral plans, operated by most undertakers, allow customers to make choices about the type of funeral they want for themselves (something this book encourages), see that these arrangements will be carried through by a specific undertaker and pay for this in advance.

One of the additional benefits of such schemes is that a funeral is bought at today's prices but delivers something that will cost more in the future. Since 1992 funeral costs have risen by nearly 75 per cent; that is far above inflation. A large proportion of these costs, however, will not be covered by most prepaid schemes as the rise is largely due to disbursements, which are beyond a funeral director's control (disbursements are the fees set by crematoria, ministers and doctors). Also excluded from most prepaid schemes are the costs of such things as flowers, obituary notices, church heating, etc. Nevertheless prepaid schemes can offer value for money since undertakers' costs could well rise faster than inflation. While you, or your inheritors, may lose the benefits that might have been gained by investing the money in a building society or in stocks and shares, prepaid schemes do have some clear benefits. They allow you to shop around for the best deal, comparing prices. This is something that your relatives are unlikely to do after your death, before arranging your funeral. Advance payment also reduces a person's capital and this may be of benefit if the person was seeking entitlement to social security benefits or hoped to keep the value of their estate under the inheritance tax threshold.

The information in this chapter was partly compiled using the <www.moneyextra.com> website. Websites like this are useful ways of finding out the latest rules and regulations concerning financial matters. As in all things, however, no website ought to be taken as the final word on financial advice and they should, therefore, be used in conjunction with professional advice from a human being sitting in front of you!

CHAPTER SIX

Funeral Directors and
Other Practicalities

As we have seen in earlier chapters, making decisions after someone has died is unlike making decisions at other points in our
lives. After most deaths, decisions have to be made quickly and
there is little time for reflection and consideration of the choices
that need to be made. One of the main reasons for writing this
book has been to try to help our readers see that a good deal of
the planning and thinking through the practicalities surrounding
death can be made before actions are necessary. After someone
has died you will often hear phrases such as 'I just want to get the
funeral over with', or a little later 'I felt as if I was in limbo until
we had got through the funeral.' Behind such statements there is
a recognition that the practicalities surrounding funerals can
often hold up the emotional side of death. Often people can feel
that they do not have the time to grieve properly while there
is so much paperwork and administration to be got through
concerning the death.

While many of the practicalities and paperwork that need to be
got through after a death can be done by most capable individuals,
it is more convenient, easier and swifter to involve professionals to
organize things at this time. In recognition of this, most people
choose to use the services of a funeral director to assist them
through this complex and emotionally fragile time.

Choosing a funeral director

The first funeral director, as we would recognize it, in the UK
was William Boyce who began trading in 'ye Grate Ould Bayley,

near Newgate' in 1675 and who was soon followed into business by William Russell in 1680, also in London. Many others who subsequently called themselves undertakers (because they 'undertook' to make the funeral arrangements on someone else's behalf) were cabinetmakers, carpenters or builders who made coffins as part of their work. As late as the 1950s in England it was still quite usual for carpenters in building firms to produce coffins for funerals. Although this practice is still quite common in Ireland, in the UK nearly all coffins today are mass-produced and bought ready-made by funeral directors. During the Victorian period there was a growing importance put on the trade of undertaking when the Metropolitan Interment Act of 1850 closed urban churchyards and, later, when cremation began in 1885. The first trade association, the British Institute of Undertakers, was founded in the late 1890s and the first qualification, the Diploma in Funeral Directing, was introduced in 1959.

Most UK undertakers (who since the middle of the twentieth century have increasingly become known in the UK by the US term 'funeral directors', to the extent that the two are interchangeable) belong to one of three trade associations, all of whom have professional codes of practice. These are: the Society of Allied and Independent Funeral Directors (SAIF); the National Association of Funeral Directors (NAFD); the Funeral Standards Council (FSC). The last of these is the largest association. You should be aware that should you choose to use an undertaker who is not a member of one of these three associations then you may well find it harder to receive a satisfactory result to any complaint that you might have. Whichever individual funeral director you choose to use, in the unfortunate and unlikely event of you needing to pursue a complaint further, you can appeal to the Funeral Ombudsman, whose contact details are given in the 'Useful Addresses' chapter of this book.

As we noted earlier, most often choosing a funeral director is made at a time of distress and urgency. For this reason the client (for this is what the bereaved person is, since funeral directors are businesspeople) is little inclined to be as choosy or as thorough over this financial transaction as they might be at other times when spending money on other things. When buying a major item such as a car, or even a smaller item such as clothing, we look at the product, compare it with other similar items and weigh up value for money. In choosing a funeral director, however, we are more likely to give our custom to the first undertaker we come across. Recognizing this, the funeral industry provides for the prepaid funerals that we discussed in Chapter 5. In addition, some people choose to visit a number of funeral directors and receive itemized quotations for the type of funeral they desire. In such quotations, full costings will be given both for the fees that will have to be paid (to doctors, crematorium, minister, etc.) and for the funeral director's own services (removal of body, coffin, cars, etc.). Whether a funeral director is chosen before or after the death, an itemized breakdown of costs should be given to the client.

Choosing a place and time for the funeral

While the precise timing of the vast majority of funerals is arranged after death there are a number of decisions that can be made beforehand. Many people may have an attachment to a particular church or chapel and wish for their funeral to be held there. By virtue of the establishment of the Church of England, a person is entitled to have their funeral held in their local parish church and/or to be buried in its churchyard or burial ground if, when they died, they were living within the parish or they were a regular worshipper at the church and had their name entered on the church's electoral roll (this is effectively the church's membership list). If either of these is not the case then the funeral may be held in the church at the discretion of the vicar. Churches of other denominations, of course, will have different rules and regulations. More details of this and related matters are discussed in Chapter 7.

Throughout this book we have encouraged our readers to think through some of the practicalities and decisions of their own funerals. Taking time to visit a church, chapel or crematorium where the funeral might be held is important. Think about issues such as your emotional attachment to the place, its aesthetics, the practicalities of holding a funeral there (a funeral with 200 mourners is, for example, not easily held in a church in the middle of a field miles from anywhere) and the journey times to the place. It may be helpful too to talk to those who work at the place in which you wish your funeral to be held. The vicar or other minister of a church, a chaplain of the chapel and the staff of the crematorium will all be able to explain what is and is not possible at a particular funeral venue and this may help you see if the place is suitable for your needs. One factor that is crucial, of course, is timing. Some crematoria hold up to a dozen or so funerals a day and if you plan for a funeral to last more than the allotted 25 minutes certain changes may be needed.

Form of service

The range of practical choices that may be made regarding the funeral service is huge. In addition to choices already mentioned, such as venue as well as whether the service is followed by a burial or a cremation, there is great scope for personalizing a service through choice of music, readings and prayers. Chapter 7 is devoted to discussing the type and shape of funeral services that can be chosen, and Chapter 8 is exclusively about the music, readings and prayers that a funeral service can have.

Hearse and limousine

One of the most obvious signs of a funeral is a hearse and

accompanying limousine passing along a street. Most funeral directors own their own hearse (or hearses) to carry the coffin, and a number of limousines to transport the close family or other mourners. Some smaller firms, however, or other larger firms at busy periods, will hire the services of a limousine owner and professional driver as necessary. Most often these vehicles are modern, black cars designed for the purpose and are renewed by the funeral director every few years. There are also older vehicles that are used, such as vintage Rolls-Royces or, more unusually still, a horse-drawn hearse.

When choosing a funeral director it is easy to overlook the type and condition of the vehicles that will be supplied; yet they play an important part in the funeral ceremonial. Few mourners will want to travel to a funeral in a limousine that is dirty inside and out, and that looks and feels as if it itself is preparing shortly to go to the great scrapheap in the sky. The colour of the cars might also be considered, as some undertakers have recently been using blue and other coloured cars rather than the traditional black. Horse-drawn hearses are expensive and there are few still in existence. However, most funeral directors will have the contact details of specialist owners who can supply these rigs if required. Ordinarily the horses are brought in a horse box to the funeral director's premises, from where they are put to work pulling the hearse to the house and thence to the church/crematorium, although a long distance to the latter might make the practicalities impossible.

Pall-bearers

Related to the hearse is the question of pall-bearers. When employing the services of a funeral director and hearse it is usual to be supplied with the services of a driver and four pall-bearers. Most firms have their own pall-bearers although some employ staff at the crematorium for this purpose. Different undertakers have different uniforms and types of dress for their staff. Many funeral directors themselves continue to dress in pinstripe trousers and morning coat with a top hat, carrying a cane. Others, like most pall-bearers and chauffeurs, wear black suits, though some wear blazers or other jackets. You may choose to find pall-bearers from among family and friends. This will reduce the cost of the funeral slightly, though most people who choose this (the minority) decide for this option because it allows for involvement of certain people in the funeral. Whatever option you choose here, it is vital that those involved feel confident in bearing the coffin and that you do not choose two giants and two midgets for the task! Even if you choose to provide your own pall-bearers, it will still be necessary for the funeral director to precede the coffin in any procession, since he or she will almost certainly be in attendance anyway.

Coffins

A coffin is the focal point of a funeral (a service immediately after death without a coffin is a memorial service). It is paraded through the streets in a glass-sided hearse, carried with great ceremony in the church or chapel in which the service is held and is then placed at the very centre of things for the ceremony.

Nearly all coffins used today are made from chipboard and have a wood-veneer to give the appearance of solid wood. In recent years US-style caskets have come to be used by some at funerals. Caskets are rectangular, with no taper from shoulder to head and foot as with coffins, and are generally more expensive than coffins. There are regulations as to what coffins or caskets may be made of, and most of the handles used on these are made of plastic coated with brass, rather than of solid metal. By law every coffin used at a funeral must have a nameplate giving the name of the deceased and, if desired, their dates of birth and death. Many also choose to have another symbol, such as a cross, attached to the end of the coffin. Coffins are ordinarily lined with a synthetic material although clients may choose another suitable material if they wish. Similarly, a body in a coffin is normally dressed in a one-piece gown, which leaves just the head showing. However, clients may choose to have the body dressed in perhaps some favourite clothes, although some restrictions may apply.

Two alternatives to the standard type of coffin might also be considered. In the last few years a number of undertakers have been supplying cardboard or wickerwork coffins to those who choose them. These can cost as much as chipboard coffins and although they are advertised as 'biodegradable' it seems to be overlooked by some that chipboard and solid wood are also biodegradable! One drawback with cardboard coffins is that if they get significantly wet over a period of time at a funeral they can become a little flexible and this can be distressing to mourners (although they do not usually get sufficiently wet to become a problem and it should certainly not be a problem at cremations). Details of how to obtain a cardboard coffin can be obtained from the Natural Death Centre, whose details are given in the 'Useful Addresses' chapter of this book. Another alternative is a reusable coffin. Here a cardboard inner coffin houses the body and a wooden outer shell covers this. When the time for cremation or burial comes, the outer shell is removed and the inner cardboard coffin is cremated or buried. This relatively new practice is in fact not so new, since in former centuries a 'parish coffin' was used to carry paupers to their funeral and the body, wrapped in a shroud, was then removed from this for burial.

Embalming

Many people, when they hear the term embalming, think that it is a process similar to that carried out on the mummies of ancient Egypt or on the bodies of Communist rulers which are to be on view after their death. In fact embalming simply means draining the blood from the veins and arteries of the body and replacing this with a preserving fluid (usually some kind of formaldehyde). The process temporarily delays the decomposition of the body by a few days and allows mourners to view the body before the funeral without the shock of seeing the person looking utterly different from how they appeared in life.

If there is not to be a viewing of the body, embalming should not be necessary. Bodies are kept in cold storage when not being viewed and this is usually sufficient to keep the body in a reasonable condition until the funeral (providing the funeral is no longer than a week or so after death). In the USA, though not required by law, nearly every body is embalmed after death. In the UK there is a greater resistance to the process, partly because the tradition of an open coffin/casket at the funeral is not so popular here, and increasingly on environmental grounds. Embalming fluid is highly toxic and many feel unhappy about the thought of pints of these chemicals going into the ground at burial or, at the very least, being released into the atmosphere. Some undertakers embalm all the bodies that they handle while others (the majority) ask before carrying out this process. It is always best at ask what the practice is and to make your own requests clear.

Organ donation

Organ donation has been one of the great successes of the last 50 years in medical research. Nevertheless as a medical procedure its widespread use has been restricted by the relatively small number of people willing to donate their organs for the use of others after their own death. It is now commonplace for the following organs to be used for donation: skin, livers, hearts, heart valves, pancreases and kidneys. In addition, each year in the UK thousands of people benefit from a cornea transplant.

Should you be willing to donate your organs for the benefit of others after your death (or, if you wish, some of them), you will need to register this intent. Your organ cannot be donated by another after you death. Not all organs that are offered for donation are accepted. Acceptance depends upon the age and condition of the organs; the donor must have been free from major infection and be HIV-, hepatitis B- and C-negative. Use of organs will also depend upon the blood suitability of the recipient. All driving licences issued since 1992 in the UK have an organ donor form enclosed. In addition to carrying this, it is preferable also to register with the NHS Organ Donor Register. The details on how to do this are given in the 'Useful Addresses' chapter of this book.

Medical research (body donation)

In order to train future doctors and other healthcare professionals in their work, a few hundred bodies are needed each year for use in medical education and research. As with organ donation, no one can make this decision for you or donate on your behalf. Those who wish their body to be used in such a way after their death should either contact their GP in the first instance, who will be able to refer them to the appropriate authority, or contact HM Inspector of Anatomy, who will direct them to the anatomy department of the nearest medical school. Contact details are given in the 'Useful Addresses' chapter of this book.

It cannot be assumed that a willingness to donate and completion of the relevant forms means that a body will be used in this way. Use of a body in medical education and research will depend upon the condition of the body at the time of death and the local demand at the medical school. The Anatomy Act allows for a body to be used by the medical school for up to three years, after which the body must be released back to the next of kin who may then arrange for a funeral to be held. If you are thinking therefore of donating your body you should also consider what service, if any, you wish to be held around the time of your death. Since it is not possible to hold a funeral at this time (because there is no body/coffin on which to focus) many people arrange for a memorial service to be held instead. As with a funeral the choice of music, readings and prayers can make this a very special occasion. It gives the mourners a chance to make a formal, and liturgical, goodbye. Many medical schools also organize an annual service of thanksgiving for those who have given their bodies for medical education and research to which families and friends of the donors are invited. If no memorial service has been held, such a service, attended also by medical students and staff, gives people a chance to mark and give thanks for the life of the donor whom they have known and loved.

Flowers and charity donations

A choice needs to be made as to whether flowers are to be had at a funeral. If they are, the funeral director will need to know so that proper arrangements can be made. The funeral notice (see below) can give the funeral director's address to which flowers may be sent. He will then ensure that the flowers are carried to the church or crematorium with the coffin. Flowers can be wreaths arranged by a florist or bouquets or other types of bunches. Once here the funeral director will ask if any of the flowers are to be placed on top of the coffin for the funeral service or whether they are simply to be laid out for mourners to see afterwards. You will also need to decide what is to happen to the flowers after the service. Some mourners choose to take at least some of the flowers, other choose to leave them in the church or crematorium or their grounds, while yet others ask for them to be taken to a local social centre or old people's home (some homes though do not like such offers as they feel as if the residents are being reminded of their own mortality!). If the flowers are left or taken away most funeral directors will, as a matter of course, collect the cards that accompany them and give them to the chief mourner.

Some people decide to ask for no flowers at the funeral. This is most often because they wish for the money that would otherwise be spent on the flowers to be given to a charity instead. Funeral directors will collect this money and pass it on to the charity. While such an intention is laudable, it should also be recognized that some people like to (perhaps, we might say, need to) make a tangible expression of their love and affection for the deceased, and flowers are one way for them to do this.

Monumental masons

While any decisions concerning what type, if any, of memorial the deceased person should have do not have to be made immediately after death, it is worth knowing something of the options available. The options are so varied that we deal with them in a separate chapter, Chapter 9. For the meantime, however, it is enough to say that some funeral directors have stone masons working within their organization while others have arrangements with local, independent masons to carry out work on their behalf. Some funeral directors (though these are few) do not deal with memorials or headstones at all.

Obituary notices

Announcements of death can be made in local and national newspapers. If the person who has died is famous in some way or another, newspapers will often publish an obituary. This does not just give the fact that the person has died but also gives details of their life and its achievements. Most of us, however, will not receive such attention and mention of the death in the press will have to be paid for. At the time of writing the cost of a simple few lines in a local newspaper is about £50 and roughly three times this amount for a national newspaper. Newspapers do not usually accept the wording for press notices by telephone, but insist upon written confirmation of what is to be published. This is because the system is then less open to distressing hoaxes and because typographical errors can be embarrassing (there was, for instance, the press notice that had a single letter mistyped in the obituary and thus it read, 'To a very dead Dad'). Such press notices may give the person's full name, age and date of death, as well as details of when and where the funeral is to be held and the address of the funeral directors, in case mourners wish to send flowers or make a donation to charity in lieu of this. Many newspapers have a standard form of words for these announcements. It is advisable not to include the address of the deceased in the press as there have been many instances of burglaries occurring while the funeral is taking place. If they wish to restrict the attendance at the funeral, some families state 'private funeral service' as part of the press announcement. It is increasingly common too for those placing the announcement to include a poem or a sentence or two relating to the deceased.

Cremated remains (ashes)

If the churchyard surrounding the church in which a funeral takes place is full, or if the deceased has chosen not to be buried, certain choices will need to be made regarding the cremated remains (ashes) of the deceased. When arrangements for the funeral are being made the funeral director will ask what the clients would like done with the ashes. Most crematoria will have the ashes ready for collection on the day following the funeral. Ashes are not normally posted to the next of kin but they should be collected personally by them or, for a fee, the funeral director will collect them. Most crematoria will also hold or store ashes for you if you wish (again, for a fee).

Ashes may be scattered or buried in a churchyard or crematorium grounds or may be taken away by the next of kin or executor of the will to be disposed of elsewhere. There is no law regulating what may or may not be done with cremated remains except that they should be stored or disposed of respectfully. Many crematoria can arrange for ashes to be buried in a special

Garden of Remembrance or scattered under a tree or in a flowerbed. Here there may be an opportunity to later place a plaque or small headstone giving details of the deceased. Many churches also have similar arrangements. In both the grounds of crematoria and in churchyards there are sometimes family plots where generations of the same family are buried or have their cremated remains placed. It is possible, even with family plots that are centuries old, to have cremated remains interred in a grave that is also a burial plot for coffins. Churches are required to keep a record of which cremated remains are interred and where, so be sure to check with the local minister before planning such an arrangement. Some crematoria have a columbarium, which is a special room or wall with niches where urns containing cremated remains may be placed and then sealed.

Some people choose to have their ashes disposed of at sea and for this no special paperwork is required. People commonly talk of ashes being 'scattered' at sea, although this is not what always happens. Care should be taken when committing loose cremated remains to the waves, since sea winds can cause obvious difficulties and embarrassments. Cremated remains that are in a container should be in one that is biodegradable (as with disposal of ashes on land). A specially designed urn for use at sea, made of suitable material, but heavy enough to sink quickly to the bottom of the sea where it allows the ashes to disperse, is available. It is appropriately called the Neptune urn and most undertakers should be able to obtain one for you or give you details of where you may obtain one personally.

Costs

We began this chapter by considering how one might choose a funeral director. We end it by looking at what is likely to be a client's final dealing with an undertaker: payment of costs. We noted that, as with all major financial transactions, it is essential that you receive from the undertaker a written estimate of the final price to be charged together with a breakdown of the individual costs involved. Codes of practice of the various trade organizations mentioned at the beginning of this chapter require funeral directors to itemize their bills in this way. Typically a funeral director's bill should include the items listed here.

- The fee covering overheads and salaries.
- Disbursements. These are fixed fees paid by the undertaker on your behalf, on which he makes no profit. These will include charges for such things as crematorium fees, the grave-digger's fees, cost of burial plot and the minister's fees. It may also include costs for such things as music, bell-ringers, choir and press notices.
- The fee for removal and storage of the body.
- The charge for the coffin and gown.
- Special items purchased (non-standard coffin or gown, for example).
- The hearse and driver.
- Pall-bearers and limousine (and driver/s).
- Travel costs to church or crematorium.
- Extra costs (for night-time removal of a body, viewing in the undertaker's chapel of rest, embalming, ashes' urn, collection of ashes, flowers, gravestone).

You cannot be charged VAT for the services of an undertaker, the supplying of hearse and cars, crematoria, cemetery or minister's fees. Coffins or ashes' containers that are bought separately from a funeral package are subject to VAT, as are flowers, press announcements and gravestones or other memorials.

CHAPTER SEVEN

Funeral Services

It is not straightforward to talk about the content of funeral services since what people choose for their funeral service, or what is chosen for them by others, may vary greatly when compared with other funerals. We noted earlier that there has been a basic human need to mark the end of life with some ritual or ceremony. Over the thousands of years of human history about which we have some understanding and today throughout the world, the forms that funerals take are many and varied. As we noted in the Introduction to this book, when thinking about what should take place at a funeral service, truth is what works. What then is it that a funeral is meant to achieve? What is its purpose?

A funeral's purpose is varied since each is unique with a different set of circumstances leading up to it and has a different set of needs to be met by those who attend it. In the UK in the twenty-first century, however, a Christian funeral might be characterized as needing to do such various things as:

- giving thanks for a life
- commending the deceased to God
- giving an opportunity for the bereaved to express their grief
- showing the love of God, found in the life of Jesus, to the bereaved
- pausing to think of human mortality
- saying farewell
- disposing of the body.

For many previous generations in the UK, funerals took place in the church of the parish in which the person had been born, lived and died. Today people rarely live all their life in one place and the church to which they have an attachment (perhaps through marriage or other family reasons) may not be the church nearest to where they died. Today most people live in a number of places in their life and the link with the local church is not what it was for our forebears. In addition to this increased mobility and weakened attachment to a particular church building, there is also a weaker attachment to the Church as an institution, with fewer people calling themselves Christian and more people having little or no contact with the Church. This, of course, has implications when it comes to planning a funeral as, for many people, funerals together with the occasional wedding service may be the only times they attend a Christian service or meet a member of the clergy.

As we noted earlier, most funerals held in the UK today are held in crematoria chapels. Until 1884 cremation was illegal in Britain and the first crematorium to open was the following year in Woking (not, as tradition says, in Burnham and Cookham!). In 1940 just 9 per cent of all funerals were held in crematoria; today, however, 70 per cent of all funerals are held in the country's 250 crematoria. Church funerals therefore account for less than a third of all funerals. Nevertheless in this chapter we shall look first at funerals that are held in church. This is done for two main reasons. First, we devote more space to church funerals than funerals in crematoria since church funerals can give greater scope for making the service more personal and intimate. Second, readers of this book are more likely to be churchgoers than not, and thus more likely to be thinking about their funeral, or the funeral of a loved one, being held in church. At the end of this chapter we then go on to say something briefly about memorial services.

Funerals in church

The basic structure of most Christian funeral services in the UK today is broadly the same. While the liturgies of the small numbers of funerals taken according to ceremonies of the Orthodox Churches and the Society of Friends (Quakers) are different, for most others the content is: the gathering; readings and sermon; prayers; commendation and farewell; the committal; the dismissal.

The gathering

Because a funeral service is an act of Christian worship it should be approached and prepared for in an appropriate way. What is considered appropriate will differ according to individual circumstances. There is, for instance, an ancient tradition of the coffin being received into the church the night before the funeral is to take place. Though this is by no means usual today, where it does happen it may be that the coffin is sprinkled with water, as a reminder of our shared baptism, and prayers may be said, as it comes through the church door. As a further symbol of the Christian faith into which the deceased had been baptized, the lit Easter (Paschal) candle is often placed near to the coffin, reminding the congregation of Christ's presence among them and of his victory over death. For the same purpose a pall, a simple white cloth, is sometimes placed over the coffin, often by family and friends of the deceased.

When the coffin is in place (be it from the night before or on the day of the funeral itself) and the congregation is in church, the minister says an opening prayer and then an opening hymn may be sung. If it has been planned for a tribute to be given by a family member or friend this now follows. Some prayers of penitence may then be said, if desired. These prayers can be very useful to the mourners since most of us have something to regret in our dealings with every person we know. Prayers at this point in the service therefore can serve as a chance to wipe the slate clean and receive the assurance of God's forgiveness before we continue with our farewell to the departed. The gathering section finishes with a special prayer called the collect, in which the minister 'collects' up the thoughts of the whole congregation about those who have died generally and the deceased person being remembered at that time in particular.

Readings and sermon

For this section there should be at least one reading from the Bible and, if desired, further readings from either the Bible or an appropriate piece of poetry or other literature. If a reading from a non-biblical source is used, it is also possible to place this reading towards the end of the service, probably after the prayers. Both these kinds of readings give the chance for a friend or relative of the deceased to be involved in the service. If you are planning your own funeral it is important that you ask the people you have in mind if they would be happy to assist in this way. If they are not asked but simply told after death (by instructions in the will or by other written means) it may be very difficult for them to say no to the request, even if they do not feel comfortable saying yes.

The sermon at funerals has an especially important part to play. Not only is it a part, along with others, where the explicitly Christian content of the service is proclaimed but it is also the point where the minister conducting the service talks in a personal way about the deceased. In this way the minister speaks both for the Church and for the bereaved. To do this well and to enable the congregation to feel that the words they have heard have spoken for them and reflect their own, varied experiences of the deceased is a skilful art. In writing funeral sermons, many clergy are appreciative of any written material about the deceased that they can read to help prepare them. Increasingly, many church people who are planning their own funeral take time to write out a brief biography of themselves and to highlight some of the things that have been most important to them in their lives. Sermons at funerals are almost always preached by members of the clergy or other licensed preachers. If another spoken, personal remembrance is desired, either to be delivered by a family member or friend, it might be best placed at the end of the gathering section.

Prayers

Prayers are most usually led by the minister leading the service but it is perfectly possible that they can be led by another person, not necessarily ordained. Although the individual circumstances of the situation and the needs of the congregation should determine what kinds of prayers are said, it is usual that the following pattern is observed:

* thanksgiving for the life of the departed
* a prayer for those who mourn
* prayers of penitence (if not already used)
* a prayer for readiness to live in the light of eternity.

It is also appropriate for the prayers to be not simply a set of words to which all respond 'Amen' but a set of prayers with fuller responses to be made by the congregation. These prayers are usually followed by the Our Father (Lord's Prayer), unless this prayer is to be used later in the service as part of the dismissal.

Commendation and farewell

The commendation is a further prayer in which the deceased person is entrusting to God's merciful keeping. The minister who is leading the service says this prayer while standing near the coffin. If the service is attended by a small number of people it may be appropriate to ask those at the service to gather round the coffin at this point. Many Roman Catholic and Anglican funerals also have the ceremony of sprinkling the coffin with water at this stage of the service. Like the sprinkling at the beginning of the service, this action recalls the water of baptism and can be extended to be an action carried out by all those attending and not just the minister who is presiding. Some clergy also encourage the censing of the coffin with incense at this point in the service, where it is seen as symbolic of the prayers of the congregation rising up to God.

The committal

The committal is the final prayer over the coffin before the body goes to its final resting-place. This might variously be immediately to the grave, as the coffin is removed from church to be taken to the crematorium or, if already at the crematorium, as it is consigned to the flames. Some clergy, if the committal takes place at the graveside, bless the grave at this point with a short prayer and, after the coffin has been lowered into place, perhaps also sprinkle it with water and cense it. After the prayer of committal at the graveside, earth is scattered on the coffin, both by the minister and members of the immediate family. At many funerals it is increasingly common for all those present to throw a handful of earth into the grave. This acts as another physical gesture demonstrating their acceptance of the death and their part in committing the loved one to his or her final resting-place.

The dismissal

The final part of a funeral liturgy is the dismissal. There is no set form of words for this and the minister leading the service may say such prayers as he or she deems appropriate for the occasion. These might include the Our Father, the *Nunc Dimittis* (words from Luke 2.29–32) or perhaps a simple prayer of blessing over the congregation. The minister might lead the congregation in singing a prayer of dismissal.

Funerals within the Eucharist

Most funerals that take place in the UK today do not involve a communion service (also known as the Eucharist, the Mass or the Lord's Supper). This is, of course, both because most funerals take place in a crematorium chapel and because those who are regular churchgoers, and therefore most used to the service of Holy Communion, are a small minority of the country's population. Many Christians, however, plan for their own funeral to take place within such a context. Every Eucharist celebrates the life, death and resurrection of Jesus and it is therefore most appropriate that a funeral service, which celebrates the new life brought to every Christian believer, brings these two together. When the Eucharist is to be celebrated as part of the funeral it takes place between the prayers and the commendation and farewell.

Chapter 8 in this book, on the music, readings and prayers, gives suggestions applicable to a funeral to be held within the celebration of the Eucharist, although the suggestions made can equally be applied to a funeral that does not involve a communion celebration. Some sensitivity should be applied when planning a funeral service involving communion, and the religious faith, or otherwise, of the mourners should be taken into account. It might not be appropriate, for instance, for the funeral to take place within a Eucharist if most of the mourners are not churchgoers as they may feel alienated and removed from the service at the point where the congregation are invited to receive the bread and wine. In such circumstances some have suggested that it might be better for the coffin to be brought into church the night before the funeral and for the Eucharist to be celebrated that evening or the following morning before the funeral.

Funerals in crematoria

As we noted earlier, most funerals held today in the UK take place in crematoria chapels. While many people feel that the brief time allotted here is not satisfactory for a meaningful service, nevertheless a short service can be just as profound and touch the hearts of the mourners as deeply as a longer service in church detailed above. Most crematoria are set within beautiful, well-maintained grounds. Such settings can add, in a positive way, to the experience of what many feel will be a bland occasion. Although the interior of many a crematorium chapel is simply furnished this may be preferred by some, as it does not become a distraction from their feelings and the words that are spoken. Others, however, may prefer the richer symbolism that some churches can bring to the occasion.

The length of most crematoria services is 20 minutes to half an hour. When you remember that this time also needs to allow for the mourners to enter the chapel, for the coffin to be brought in and for the mourners to leave, not much time is left for the service itself. If such brevity is anticipated to become a problem it is possible, at extra cost, to book the chapel for two slots of time, perhaps then allowing for the service to be nearer an hour long. However, even with a service taking less than half an hour, a funeral in a crematorium chapel can be a wonderful occasion. The basic structure of the service will be as for the funeral in church and there will also be scope for choosing hymns (though only one or, perhaps, two), a reading, a psalm and some prayers. Clergy, whose experiences of leading funeral services is mostly based on crematoria, will be able to advise as to what will be possible given the time and other constraints. It is entirely possible, for instance, that such things as the symbolism of sprinkling the coffin or placing Christian symbols on the coffin can be done in the same way as if the funeral were taking place in church.

Memorial services

A memorial service, like a cremation, is a relatively modern phenomenon in the UK. The first recorded memorial service was that held after the death of Princess Charlotte, the 20-year-old only child of George IV (and therefore heir to the throne) in

1817. The widespread national mourning felt at this time was replicated in 1852 when memorial services were held throughout the country to coincide with the funeral of the Duke of Wellington in St Paul's Cathedral. Nine years later similar services were held to remember the life of Prince Albert, Queen Victoria's husband.

Today there may be a variety of reasons for considering having a memorial service after death. Most memorial services are held in church rather than crematoria chapels or other places. A memorial service might be held in addition to a funeral if the funeral was being held far from where the memorial service was to be held. A person might, for instance, have died at one end of the country but until recently lived hundreds of miles away and thus friends want to remember her there. A memorial service might also be held if the church or chapel where the funeral was held was too small to accommodate all those who wanted to attend (this may be the case when a public figure dies or in the case of the death of a young person). Those who give their body for medical education and research might have a memorial service held for them soon after death since their body will have been removed to the medical school and there is no possibility of a funeral being held.

All these reasons, together with others, may be good and valid reasons for holding a memorial service. Remember that in dealing with grief and thanksgiving for a life, truth is what works. Rarely, however, do memorial services meet a need if they are held too long after the time of death (say, more than two months). This is because, like funerals, memorial services are part of the grieving process. If the memorial service is unduly delayed the service may not be meeting the needs of the congregation in such an obvious or helpful way. If it is to be held much later, then the readings, prayers, music and sermon should all reflect the fact that the grief of the mourners has moved on and is almost certainly not felt as sharply as immediately after the death.

The wake

In many countries of the world the mourners at a funeral will gather together before the service to remember the loved one who has died. This meeting often begins at the time that the coffin is received into church the night before the funeral and a vigil until the following day begins. For this reason it is often called a 'wake' since those gathered are staying awake until the service itself. At such a gathering people may talk privately or publicly about the deceased as they share their memories, mourn the person's passing and receive the love and support of the Christian community that has come together. The wake takes place most often in the home of the deceased or in the home of a close relative. In the UK today such a wake is rare, though many hold a gathering with a similar purpose after the service.

CHAPTER EIGHT

Music, Readings and Prayers

Thus far this book has for the large part been concerned with the practicalities of the preparation of legal, financial and other matters. All this of course is vital in ensuring that what happens after death is what was intended by the person who has died. However, this book is a *funeral* handbook and it is to suggestions for the content of the funeral service itself that we now turn. We have looked in previous chapters at the settings for such a service and at the order that such a service may take. We have seen how a large part of a funeral service is prescribed by the various Christian denominations (though we saw too that there was scope for adaptation) and that certain elements are regarded as essential when putting together a funeral liturgy. There is, though, much else in the service that can be chosen and person-alized by either the person whose funeral it is or those arranging the funeral. All this is best done in consultation with the priest or minister who is to lead the service.

Through the choice of music, readings and prayers the mood of the service can be set and certain themes can be emphasized. The funeral service itself is probably the one and only chance for certain things to be said and given prominence in the whole of the bereavement process. It is almost certain that only at the funeral will family and friends of the deceased be gathered together in one place at the same time. Through advanced choice of music, readings and prayers the deceased person can share with all these people exactly what the tone of their remembrance might be. For instance one person, in planning his own funeral, created a chance for people both to pause to reflect on the shortness of human life and to smile when he chose the song

Je ne regrette rien as part of his service. Appropriate use of the opportunity given by music, readings and prayers also allows the possibility of certain family members and friends of the deceased to take an active part in the service either by reading aloud or leading the prayers. Some people are also lucky enough to have friends who are musically accomplished and who would be delighted to be asked to use their talents during the service. Organists, singers and other musicians can all participate in such a way, if desired.

Music

There are a numbers of points during a funeral service when music is appropriate. This may be either organ music, music played on a number of other instruments, hymns sung by all the members of congregation or perhaps music sung by a choir or a soloist. Music may be performed before, during and after the service. Organ music can be played before the service starts while the congregation assemble and at the end of the service as they depart (though most organists would prefer the congregation to remain in their seats and listen to the music that they have spent time practising). It is also quite common for there to be a point where the congregation listen to some music being played. This may be an anthem sung by a choir, a piece of music played by a soloist or a group of musicians or, increasingly, perhaps a piece of recorded music played from a CD or tape.

Processional

The music that is played before and at the beginning of a service can have a crucial role in setting the tone for the rest of the funeral itself. Depending on the feeling that you want the funeral to convey, quiet or loud, serious or lighter music might variously be appropriate. During the actual service (as it begins in fact), people often choose to have some music played as the coffin is carried into church, preceded by the priest. The following pieces of music, many for organ, express a whole range of different modes and feelings. Many might well also be as appropriately played (or perhaps more so) at the end of the service. Some of the pieces were written for orchestra or strings but can be found in adaptations for organ. As with music before the service, some of these pieces will most easily be played on CD or tape.

- Albinoni – Adagio in G minor
- J. S. Bach – Cantata No. 208, No. 9, *Schafe konnen sicher weiden* (Sheep may safely graze)
- J. S. Bach – Cantata No. 147, No. 10, *Jesu bleibet meine Freude* (Jesu, joy of man's desiring)
- J. S. Bach – Toccata and Fugue in D minor
- Barber – Adagio for strings
- Beethoven – Piano Concerto No. 4, first movement
- Beethoven –Symphony No. 6, last movement
- Beethoven –Violin Concerto in D minor, second movement
- Brahms – Symphony No. 3, last movement
- Britten – *Simple Symphony*, third movement (Sentimental Sarabande)
- Chopin – Nocturne No. 8 in D flat
- Chopin – Prelude No. 4 in E minor
- Chopin – Sonata No. 2 in B flat minor (Funeral Sonata)
- Copland – *Fanfare for the Common Man*
- Debussy – *Suite Bergamasque*, No. 3, *Clair de lune*
- Debussy – Prelude No. 8, *La fille aux cheveux de lin* (The girl with the flaxen hair)
- Delius – *A Village Romeo and Juliet*, No. 19, The Walk to the Paradise Garden
- Dvorak – Symphony No. 9, 'From the New World', second movement (Going home)
- Elgar – Variations on an Original Theme, 'Enigma', No. 9, Nimrod

- Elgar – Serenade, second movement
- Elgar – Symphony No. 1, first movement
- Elgar – Symphony No. 2, slow movement
- Grieg – *Holberg Suite*, No. 4, Air
- Grieg – *Two Elegiac Melodies*, No. 2, Last Spring
- Handel – *Water Music*, No. 1f, Air
- Haydn – *The Seven Last Words of Our Saviour on the Cross*
- Haydn – String Quartet Op. 76, No. 3 in C, 'Emperor', second movement
- Holst – *The Planets*, No. 4, Jupiter
- Karg-Elert – *Choral Improvisations*, No. 59, *Nun danket alle Gott*
- MacDowell – *Woodland Sketches*, No. 1, To a wild rose
- Mahler – Symphony No. 5, *Adagietto* (Death in Venice)
- Messaien – *L'Ascension*
- Mozart – Piano Concerto No. 21 in C, second movement (Elvira Madigan)
- Puccini – *Preludio Sinfonico*
- Ravel – *Pavane pour une infante défunte*
- Schoenberg – *Verklarte nacht*
- Schubert – String Quartet No. 14 in D minor, 'Death and the Maiden', second movement
- Schubert – Piano Sonata No. 21 in B flat, second movement
- Schubert – String Quintet in C, first and second movements
- Schubert – Impromptu No. 3 in G flat
- Schubert – Impromptu No. 4 in A flat
- Strauss – *Vier letzte lieder*, No. 4, *Im abendrot* (At sunset)
- Strauss – *Metamorphosen*
- Tavener – *The Protecting Veil*, opening
- Vaughan Williams – *Fantasia on a Theme of Thomas Tallis*
- Vaughan Williams – *The Lark Ascending*
- Wagner – *Tristan und Isolde*, No. 19, *Liebestod* (Death in love)
- Wagner – *Gotterdammerung*, No. 37 (Siegfried's funeral march)
- Widor – Symphony No. 5, Toccata

Hymns

There are a number of hymns that have been especially written with funeral services in mind, and plenty of other general hymns are well-suited to the occasion too. You might like to choose your favourite hymns or to choose hymns that have special associations. Some people, for instance, choose hymns for their funeral that were sung at their wedding or perhaps at the funeral of their partner. Why not ask your minister if you can borrow a hymn book from church, in order to look at the words of various hymns, to help you in your choice. When choosing hymns it is worth remembering that some newer or less frequently sung hymns might not be known by those attending the service and that therefore the singing of these particular hymns at the funeral might be less than hearty! Listed below are some funeral hymns and some of the most popular hymns (and therefore tried and tested) chosen for funerals.

Hymns written specifically for funerals:

- 'Brief life is here our portion'
- 'Christ, enthroned in highest heaven'
- 'Day of wrath! O day of mourning!'
- 'God be in my head'
- 'Jesus, Son of Mary'
- 'Now the labourer's task is o'er'
- 'O Lord, to whom the spirits live'
- 'What sweet of life endureth'

General hymns also suitable for funerals:

- 'Abide with me; fast falls the eventide'
- 'All things bright and beautiful'
- 'As pants the hart for cooling streams'
- 'Blest are the pure in heart'
- 'Guide me, O thou great Redeemer'

- 'He wants not friends that hath thy love'
- 'I danced in the morning'
- 'Jerusalem the golden'
- 'Jesus lives! Thy terrors now'
- 'Joy and triumph everlasting'
- 'Let saints on earth in concert sing'
- 'Lord, it belongs not to my care'
- 'Now is eternal life'
- 'Now thank we all our God'
- 'O God, our help in ages past'
- 'Praise, my soul, the King of heaven'
- 'Praise to the Holiest in the height'
- 'The day thou gavest, Lord, is ended'
- 'The King of love my shepherd is'
- 'The Lord's my shepherd, I'll not want'
- 'There is a land of pure delight'
- 'They whose course on earth is o'er'
- 'Thine be the glory, risen, conquering Son'

Psalms

If the funeral is to include a celebration of Holy Communion you have an opportunity to choose a psalm to be sung. Usually a psalm (or sometimes another hymn) is sung immediately before the reading of the Gospel or between the first and second readings. It can be sung either by the whole congregation or by a choir. To help you make your choice, look at a Bible (where the psalms are originally to be found) or a psalter (a book of psalms, set to music). The following are offered as suggestions for you to consider.

- Psalm 23
- Psalm 25.6–7, 17–18, 20–1
- Psalm 27.1, 4, 7–9, 13–14
- Psalm 42.2–3, 5

- Psalm 62.2–6, 8–9
- Psalm 103.8, 10, 13–18
- Psalm 115.1, 9–13
- Psalm 116.10–11, 15–16
- Psalm 130
- Psalm 143.1–2, 5–8, 10

Anthems

There is a wide range of choral music that may be sung as an anthem in a funeral service. The possibilities are only really restricted by the appropriateness of the piece of music to a funeral service. Here again consultation with the priest who is officiating is of great importance. Having an anthem allows for certain thoughts and feelings to be expressed by the person who chooses the music in a way which is not possible with instrumental music. With anthems it is not only the tone of music that is being conveyed but also perhaps a message is conveyed through the words. It is worth remembering that the music which is chosen as an anthem is also likely to be listened to more attentively than processional and recessional music. This is because when music is played at these points those attending the funeral are likely also to be looking at the coffin being brought in or out of church and it is likely that they may be feeling more emotional at these points. Remember too that not everyone will remain in church at the end of a funeral to hear the whole piece of music played and they may not have been at church early enough to hear all of the music played before the service either.

- Anerio – *Missa pro Defunctis, Kyrie* and *Sanctus*
- Bainton – And I saw a new heaven
- Bairstow – Jesu, grant me this I pray
- Bairstow – Save us, O Lord
- Byrd – *Ave verum corpus*
- Byrd – Four-part Mass, *Agnus Dei*

- Byrd – Gradualia Vol. 1, *Iustorum animae*
- Byrd – Short Service, *Nunc Dimittis*
- Croft – Funeral Sentences, Burial Service
- Elgar – *Ave verum corpus*
- Gibbons – Almighty and everlasting God
- Gibbons – First (short) Service, *Nunc Dimittis*
- Goss – O Saviour of the world
- Goss – O taste and see how gracious the Lord is
- Harris – Bring us, O Lord God
- Harris – *Evening Hymn*
- Harris – Faire is the heaven
- Howells – Take him, earth, for cherishing
- Ireland – Greater love hath no man than this
- Morley – Short Service, *Nunc Dimittis*
- Mozart – *Ave verum corpus*
- Palestrina – *Missa Brevis, Agnus Dei*
- Parry – *Songs of Farewell*
- Parsons – *Ave Maria*
- Phillips – Christ in Five Parts, *Ave verum corpus*
- Rutter – God be in my head
- Stainer – *The Crucifixion*, No. 5, God so loved the world
- Stanford – Services in B flat, *Nunc Dimittis*
- Stanford – Three Motets, No. 1, *Justorum animae*
- Stanford – Three Motets, No. 3, *Beati quorum via*
- Tallis – If ye love me, keep my commandments
- Tavener – *Funeral Ikos*
- Tomkins – Third Service, *Nunc Dimittis*
- Walford Davies – God be in my head
- Walford Davies – *Solemn Melody*
- Walmisley – Evening Service in D minor, *Nunc Dimittis*
- Walton – Drop, drop slow tears
- Walton – Where does the uttered music go?
- S. S. Wesley – Let us lift up our heart
- S. S. Wesley – Man that is born of woman
- S. S. Wesley - Thou wilt keep him in perfect peace

Recessional music

Like the music played before the service begins, the music played at the end of a funeral can have an important part to play in the grief of the mourners. Some people will want quiet, unobtrusive music played both before and after the service while others might choose a more upbeat piece of music on which to end the service, expressing the Christian belief in the resurrection. A wide range of music for the end of the service is therefore possible. The choices here are similar to those for the processional music and therefore no separate list is necessary.

Other music

Although most music that is played or sung in funeral services in church is played or sung live, much of the music at funerals that take place in crematoria is now played on a sound system via CD or tape. It is possible too for such music to be played at funerals in church. Music played in this way has become popular for a number of reasons. Perhaps an organist or choir is not always available. Perhaps it is impractical for reasons of cost, size of church or other practicalities to have certain pieces of music performed live (for instance, your church and your wallet may not be able to accommodate the London Symphony Orchestra!). Music chosen from CD or tape also has the advantage of a certain level of performance being guaranteed. This recorded music may be appropriate at any of the various points discussed earlier in this chapter. As with more 'traditional' music, it is always best that the music is arranged in consultation with and at the discretion of the priest. The list of possible music to be played here is almost endless and it might be overtly 'religious' or 'secular'. As music from the former category has been discussed and suggested above and music from the latter category is highly personal, it is not necessary to provide a list of suggestions at this point. The increasing acceptance and popularity of 'secular' music can be seen by the positive reaction by many to the music at the funeral of Diana, Princess of Wales, which included music such as Elton John's 'Candle in the Wind.'

Readings

As we saw in Chapter 7, 'Funeral Services', there is scope for one or more readings from the Bible to be chosen to be read at a funeral service. In the section below we offer some suggestions, which you might like to consider using. Each Bible reference is followed by a very brief description of what the passage chosen is about. It is a good idea to get a copy of a modern translation of the Bible and read through the passages suggested. There will be some passages that appeal to some people and different passages that appeal to others. This is fine. Choose the reading or readings that most reflect what you feel about the Christian faith and its hope and which you want to share with others at the funeral. You might like to look at more than one translation of a passage as this might give a different feel or emphasis to the reading. We suggest that you begin by consulting the New Revised Standard Version of the Bible.

Old Testament and Apocrypha
- *Genesis 42.29–38*
  The sorrow you would cause would kill me.
- *2 Samuel 1.17, 23–6*
  David's lament for Saul and Jonathan.
- *2 Samuel 12.16–23*
  David's son dies.
- *Job 19.1, 23–7*
  This I know: that my Redeemer lives.
- *Isaiah 25.6–9*
  The Lord will destroy death for ever.
- *Isaiah 53.1–10*
  The suffering servant.

- *Isaiah 61.1–3*
  To comfort all those who mourn.
- *Lamentations 3.17–26*
  Wait in silence, for the love of the Lord never comes to an end.
- *Daniel 12.1–3, 5–9*
  Those who lie sleeping in the dust will awake, for their names
  are written in the book.
- *Wisdom 3.1–9*
  The souls of the righteous are in the hands of God.
- *Wisdom 4.7–15*
  Age is not length of time, but an untarnished life.
- *Ecclesiasticus 38.16–23*
  Do not forget that there is no coming back.
- *2 Maccabees 12.43–5*
  A fine and noble action, in which he took account of the
  resurrection.

Psalms

- Psalm 6
- Psalm 23
- Psalm 25
- Psalm 27
- Psalm 32
- Psalm 38.9–22
- Psalm 39
- Psalm 42
- Psalm 90
- Psalm 116
- Psalm 118.4–29
- Psalm 120
- Psalm 121
- Psalm 130
- Psalm 138
- Psalm 139

New Testament (Epistles and other readings)

- *Romans 5.6–11*
  Having died to make us righteous, is it likely that Christ would now fail to save us from God's anger?
- *Romans 5.17–21*
  However great the number of sins committed, grace was even greater.
- *Romans 6.3–9*
  All of those who have been baptized into Jesus Christ were baptized into his death.
- *Romans 8.14–23*
  The future glory: we wait for our bodies to be set free.
- *Romans 8.31–9*
  Nothing can come between us and the love of God.
- *Romans 14.7–12*
  Whether we are living or dead, we belong to the Lord.
- *1 Corinthians 15.20–3*
  All will be brought to life in Christ.
- *1 Corinthians 15.20–58*
  The resurrection of the dead: death is swallowed up in victory.
- *2 Corinthians 4.7–15*
  We carry in our mortal bodies the death of Jesus.
- *2 Corinthians 4.16—5.10*
  Visible things only last for a while, but the invisible is eternal.
- *2 Corinthians 5.1, 6–10*
  We have an everlasting home in heaven.
- *Ephesians 3.14–21*
  The power to understand Christ's love.
- *Philippians 3.10–21*
  God's purpose for all of us, in which we will be transformed.
- *1 Thessalonians 4.13–18*
  So we shall always be with the Lord.
- *2 Timothy 2.8–13*
  If we have died with him, we shall also live with him.

- *1 Peter 1.3–9*
  We have been born anew to a living hope.
- *1 John 3.1–3*
  We shall see him as he really is and shall be like him.
- *1 John 3.14–16*
  We have passed out of death and into life because we love those around us.
- *Revelation 7.9–17*
  The crowd worshipping in heaven.
- *Revelation 21.1–7*
  Behold, I make all things new.
- *Revelation 21.22–7; 22.3b–5*
  The Lord God will be their light.

New Testament (Gospel readings)

- *Matthew 5.1–12*
  Rejoice and be glad, for your reward will be great in heaven.
- *Matthew 11.25–30*
  Come to me, and I will give you rest.
- *Matthew 25.31–46*
  The final judgement. Come, you who the Father has blessed.
- *Mark 10.13–16*
  Let the little children come to me.
- *Mark 15.33–9; 16.1–6*
  He has risen, he is not here.
- *Luke 7.11–17*
  Young man, I tell you to get up.
- *Luke 12.35–40*
  The coming of the Son of Man: stand ready.
- *Luke 23.33, 39–43*
  Today you will be with me in paradise.
- *Luke 24.1–11*
  The resurrection.
- *Luke 24.13–35*

Was it not ordained that Christ should suffer and enter into his glory?

- *John 5.19–29*
  Whoever hears my word and believes him who sent me, has eternal life.
- *John 6.35–40*
  Whoever believes in the Son has eternal life, and I shall raise him up on the last day.
- *John 6.51–8*
  Anyone who eats this bread has eternal life, and I shall raise him up at the last day.
- *John 11.17–27*
  I am the resurrection and the life.
- *John 11.32–45*
  Lazarus is raised from the dead.
- *John 12.23–8*
  If a grain of wheat dies, it yields a rich harvest.
- *John 14.1–6*
  There are many rooms in my Father's house.
- *John 17.24–6*
  I want them to be where I am.
- *John 19.17–18, 25b–30*
  Bowing his head he gave up his spirit.
- *John 19.38–42*
  The burial of Christ.
- *John 20.1–11*
  The resurrection of Christ.

Other readings

As well as having a reading or two from the Bible it may be that there is a particular piece of prose or a poem that could be read at the funeral. Those planning their own funeral might want to share a favourite piece of literature, which has meant a lot to them in their life, with their family and friends. Those who are organizing the funeral of another person might want to use the opportunity of a reading from somewhere other than the Bible to offer words of comfort to others. Whatever the reason for choosing such a piece, as with all other parts of the funeral, it is important that the piece reflects something of the deceased or is directed towards the needs of the mourners. We offer the following four readings in full – the first is often used at funerals – for you to consider as examples of the kinds of readings for funerals that can be suitably used but which do not come from the Bible. All four of these pieces have a theme: that of a continuing presence of the loved one beyond the grave. They show the variety of poetry and prose that can be used in funerals. Continuing presence is, of course, only one theme and there are others that you might like to explore including: consolation, eternal life, celebration, thanks, reconciliation, faith, hope and love.

Death is nothing at all. I have only slipped away into the next room. I am I and you are you. Whatever we were to each other that we are still. Call me by my old familiar name, speak to me in the easy way which you always used. Put no difference in your tone; wear no forced air of solemnity or sorrow. Laugh as we always laughed at the little jokes we enjoyed together. Play, smile, think of me, pray for me. Let my name be spoken without effort, without the ghost of a shadow on it. Life means all that it ever meant. It is the same as it ever was; there is absolutely unbroken continuity. Why should I be out of mind because I am out of sight? I am waiting for you for an interval, somewhere very near, just around the corner. All is well.

'Death is Nothing at All', Henry Scott Holland

I am standing upon that foreshore. A ship at my side spreads her white sails in the morning breeze and starts for the blue ocean. She is an object of beauty and strength and I stand and watch her until at length she hangs like a speck of white cloud just where the sea and sky come down to mingle with each other. Then someone at my side says, 'There! She is gone!' 'Gone where?' 'Gone from my sight, that's all.' She is just as large in mast and spar and hull as ever she was when she left my side; just as able to bear her load of living freight to the place of her destination. Her diminished size is in me, not in her. And just at that moment when someone at my side says, 'There! She is gone!' there are other eyes watching her coming and other voices ready to take up the glad shout, 'Here she comes!' And that is dying.

'The Ship' (from *Toilers of the Sea*), Victor Hugo

Remember me when I have gone away,
Gone far away into the silent land;
When you can no more hold me by the hand,
nor I half turn to go yet turning stay.
Remember me when no more day by day
you tell me of our future that you planned:
Only remember me; you understand
it will be late to counsel then or pray.
Yet if you should forget me for a while
and afterwards remember, do not grieve:
For if the darkness and corruption leave
a vestige of the thoughts that once I had,
better by far you should forget and smile
than that you should remember and be sad.

'Remember', Christina Rossetti

Music, when soft voices die,
vibrates in the memory;
Odours, when sweet violets sicken,
live within the sense they quicken.

Rose leaves, when the rose is dead,
are heaped for the beloved's bed;

And so thy thoughts, when thou art gone,
love itself shall slumber on.

'Music', Percy Bysshe Shelley

Prayers

As with the readings, the kinds of prayers that are used at a funeral
will help convey the sense in which the deceased person wished
to be remembered. There is a world of difference, for instance,
between a prayer that is said to remember a person tragically
killed unexpectedly and a prayer for a person who knew death
was coming and had prepared himself or herself and those
around for this. In this final section of this chapter we suggest
some different topics or themes for prayer, which you may like
to consider when planning a funeral. Every funeral is different
because every human life is different but human experience is
often very similar. Because of this, one prayer is given for each
theme. We hope that the themes listed will help you think about
the tone of the funeral you are planning and the suitability, or
otherwise, of the different kinds of prayer to be used in the
service. Please remember that the priest or minister leading the
service will have certain prayers which she will want to use. Why
not talk to whoever will be taking the service and ask for advice
about what would help make a good set of prayers?

Bidding (opening prayer)

O Lord, support us all the day long of this troublous life, until
the shades lengthen and the evening comes, and the busy
world is over and our work is done. Then, Lord, in your mercy,
grant us a safe lodging, a holy rest and peace at the last;
through Jesus Christ our Lord. Amen.

Grief

O God of grace and glory, we give you thanks for giving
(*name*) to us to know and love as a companion on our earthly

94

pilgrimage. In your boundless compassion, console all who mourn; give us faith to see in death the gate of eternal life, so that, in quiet confidence we may continue on earth, until by your call, we are united with those who have gone before; through Jesus Christ our Lord. Amen.

Remembrance

Grant, O Lord, that keeping in glad remembrance those who have gone before, who have stood by us and helped us, who have cheered us by their sympathy and strengthened us by their example, we may seize every opportunity of life and rejoice in the promise of a glorious resurrection with them, through Jesus Christ our Lord. Amen.

Thanksgiving

God our Father, we thank you that you have made each one of us in your own image, and given us gifts and talents with which to serve you. We thank you for (*name*), the joys and trials we shared together, the good we saw in *him/her*, the love we received from *him/her*. Now give us strength and courage to leave *him/her* in your care, confident in your promise of eternal life, through Jesus Christ our Lord. Amen.

Consolation

Father of mercies and God of all consolation, you pursue us with untiring love and dispel the shadow of death with the bright dawn of life. Comfort your family in their loss and sorrow. Be our refuge and our strength, O Lord, and lift us from the depths of grief into the peace and light of your presence. Your Son, our Lord Jesus Christ, by dying has destroyed our death, and by rising, restored our life. Enable us therefore to press on toward him, so that, after our earthly course is run, he may reunite us with those we love, when every tear will be wiped away. We ask this through Christ our Lord. Amen.

95

Petition

Bring us, O Lord God, at our last awakening into the house and gate of heaven, to enter into that gate, and dwell in that house, where there shall be no darkness or dazzling, but one equal light; no noise or silence, but one equal music; no fears nor hopes, but one equal possession; no ends nor beginnings, but one equal eternity; in the habitation of your glory and dominion, world without end. Amen.

Mercy

Into your hands, O Lord, we humbly entrust our beloved *brother/sister (name)*. In this life you embraced *him/her* with your tender love; deliver *him/her* from every evil and bid *him/her* enter eternal rest. The old order has passed away: welcome *him/her* then into paradise, where there will be no sorrow, no weeping nor pain, but the fullness of peace and joy with your Son and the Holy Spirit for ever and ever. Amen.

Penitence

God our Redeemer, you love all that you have made, you are merciful beyond our deserving. Pardon your servant's sins, acknowledged and unperceived. Help us also to forgive as we pray to be forgiven, through him who on the cross asked forgiveness of those who wounded him. Amen.

Peace

Lord, make me a channel of thy peace; where there is hatred may I bring love; where there is injury, pardon; where there is doubt, faith; where there is despair, hope; where there is darkness, light; and where there is sadness, joy. O Divine Master, grant that we may not so much seek to be consoled as to console; to be understood as to understand; to be loved as to love; for it is in giving that we receive, it is in pardoning that we are pardoned, and it is in dying that we are born to eternal life. Amen.

Commendation

Give rest, O Christ, to your servant with thy saints: where sorrow and pain are no more; neither sighing, but life everlasting. You only art immortal, the Creator and Maker of all: and we are mortal, formed of the earth, and unto earth shall we return as you ordained, when you created us saying, 'Dust you are, and to dust you shall return.' We all go down to the dust: and weeping at the grave we make our song: alleluia, alleluia, alleluia.

Committal

Forasmuch as it has pleased Almighty God of his great mercy to take unto himself the soul of our dear *brother/sister* (*name*) we therefore commit *his/her* body to the ground; earth to ashes, dust to dust; in sure and certain hope of the resurrection to eternal life through Jesus Christ our Lord. Amen.

Closing prayer

May the road rise up to meet you, may the wind be always at your back, may the sun shine warm upon your face, the rain fall soft upon your fields, until we meet again, may God hold you in the palm of his hand. Amen.

Blessing

Go forth into the world in peace, be strong and of good courage, hold fast that which is good. Love and serve the Lord with singleness of heart, rejoicing in the power of the Holy Spirit and may the blessing of God Almighty, the Father, the Son and the Holy Spirit be upon you this day and always. Amen.

CHAPTER NINE

Memorials

It is natural that many people, after the death of a loved one, will want to make some kind of physical expression of their love for the deceased person. This is, of course, the role that a funeral fulfils for most people. Even the simplest of funerals gives some ritual or rite, which enables those who are bereaved to show in actions what their words cannot express. Even the simple action where a coffin is carried into a church or chapel with reverence does this. The clothes that are worn by mourners can be important for many people, signifying either the solemnity of mourning or the joy of thanksgiving for a life well lived. During the service itself there may be flowers on the coffin, the coffin may be sprinkled with water, people may bow towards the coffin and candles – symbolizing the prayers that have been said for the deceased – may be lit. All these things are part of the process of remembering and giving thanks for the person's life and are, too, as we have already said, part of the process of healing which is necessary after death for those left behind.

All these physical expressions of love and respect at the funeral are, in one sense, beginning to memorialize the person who has died. Though the person is no longer alive, nevertheless people wish to show that the person's life and death was important to them. Many feel that they wish to continue to express such feelings some time after the death. In their home photographs of the deceased may take on a greater prominence, for instance. Outside the home the marking of the grave with a headstone is a common and ancient way of erecting a memorial. The rest of this chapter will look at the history and various expressions of memorials, and suggest ways in which grief can be helped to be healed by memorialization taking place.

History of memorials

Remembering the dead is an important part of mourning a loved one. The phenomenon is not new, neither is it confined to any one part of the world. One only has to look at the huge number of stone circles and burial mounds that still exist in the UK today and which date from what are called by some 'the Dark Ages' to realize how there seems to be a basic human need to bury the dead with dignity and then to create a memorial by which to remember them. In Mexico today, the Day of the Dead is celebrated with families taking picnics to the graves of dead loved ones where they both talk about the deceased and clean their graves. In China there is an annual national day of mourning to visit graves, honour ancestors and remember the dead. Japan has the festival of Tor-Nagashi each August where the dead are remembered at Lake Matsue, where floating lanterns have the family name on one side and a prayer written on the other. In Brazil, on New Year's Eve, a similar ceremony takes place on Copacabana beach.

Having acknowledged these examples we can see then that remembering the dead is not a just a Western, Christian or even modern phenomenon. In the Western Christian tradition, however, the remembering of the dead has been traditionally focused especially on one particular day. In the late ninth century, Abbot Odilo of Cluny in France ordered that 2 November should be observed by members of his religious order as All Souls' Day. This local observance spread and soon became popular throughout Europe. On All Saints' Day (1 November), the Church in the West remembers all those who had such remarkable and holy lives that it regards them as saints. The following day the Church remembers all those who have died and lived a life of faith, both those whose faith was known and those who faith was known to God alone. Many churches in the UK hold special services on 2 November where names of the departed are read out as part of the liturgy. These names might be those that have been given to the priest by members of the congregation and, more generally, the names of those people who have died in the last twelve months. At such services there is often the chance to light a candle in memory of a loved one, giving physical expression to the remembrance that is taking place in the heart.

Memorials after burial

Burials in churchyards

Anyone, whether or not they are a member of the Church of England or even a Christian, who lives within the ecclesiastical parish is entitled to be buried in that parish's churchyard. There are around 16,500 parish churches in England. Because many churchyards are full and new graves cannot therefore be cut, some parishes have burial grounds that are separate from the church and which may still be open to new burials. Even where churchyards or burial grounds are full it is still likely that burials can take place in existing family graves. The incumbent of the parish (vicar, rector or priest-in-charge), together with the parochial church council, has the legal power to decide which non-parishioners may be buried in the parish's churchyard or burial ground.

A fee is payable for a burial in parish ground. The cost of this varies according to whether the burial is immediately preceded by a funeral in church. The fee paid does not give possession of the land to be used for the grave but rather the right of use only; the land remains the property of the church. This right can be passed on through a will or as part of an estate.

If you wish for a memorial, such as a headstone, to be placed on the grave after burial certain regulations control what may and may not be erected. The same regulations (those of the legal executive, the chancellor, of the diocese) specify what wording may be placed on any memorial. The incumbent of the parish has the responsibility of deciding, on the chancellor's behalf, what is permitted. It is important then to have the style of memorial, the material to be used and the wording or images which are to be placed on it agreed by the incumbent before any order is placed with the funeral director or stonemason. The incumbent will be able to steer you through successful completion of the forms for the granting of a 'faculty' (the Church's legal document, giving permission for things to be done within a church or its burial grounds). There is a fee payable before a faculty is granted.

Burials in cemeteries

Cemeteries are mostly managed either by local authorities or by private companies and there is usually little restriction as to who may be buried in cemeteries. As with church burials there is a fee to be paid, both to the owners of the cemetery and to the clergy taking the burial service. Since cemeteries are variously owned, the level of the fees payable can vary quite widely. The superintendent (the person in charge of a cemetery) will be able to advise you as to what these fees will be, though the amount payable is often higher if the deceased was not a local resident.

As with the fees paid for burial in churchyards or church burial grounds, the fees paid for burial in cemeteries does not give ownership of the land but only certain defined rights. The right might be for exclusive use of the land for a certain number of years and/or it might be for permission for more than one burial to take place in the plot. Permission was formerly granted for graves to be used 'in perpetuity' though today permission for use is rarely granted for a period longer than 50 years.

Unlike the memorials that are erected in many churchyards, many cemeteries are very restrictive in what type of gravestone or other memorial may be placed on the grave. Most cemeteries prefer 'lawn graves', which are graves that simply have a headstone and no curbing or any other marker on the grave. Such graves make maintenance of the grass simpler. Some cemeteries, however, do permit great latitude in what is used to mark a grave. In recent years the erection of a mausoleum over a grave has been granted in some cemeteries. Mausolea allow for a number of coffins to be entombed above ground and are not so dissimilar to those tombs, erected centuries ago, which can still been seen in old churchyards.

The law does not restrict burials to churchyards and cemeteries. In fact, the freeholder of any piece of land may allow burial to take place, provided certain obligations are fulfilled (burials may not take place too close to rivers or the water table, for instance). It is perfectly possible for a person to be buried in the back garden of a house. Because this is so unusual, it is wise to check with the local authority's planning department before making such plans.

Memorials after cremation

Cremated remains

Since many churchyards are full for burial, many now offer the possibility of having one's cremated remains interred in the churchyard instead. If a family grave already exists in the churchyard the ashes may be placed there but it is more common now for ashes to be placed within a special Garden of Remembrance, reserved exclusively for this use. Some churches allow small headstones with the deceased's names and dates to be placed flat on the ground over the grave, while others may make provision for names to be recorded on a larger stone at the entrance to the garden or plot. A fee is payable for all interments of cremated remains.

In cemeteries, regulations will also vary from place to place. Until perhaps 20 years ago most cremated remains were scattered or interred at cemeteries without a memorial being subsequently erected. Gradually, however, more cemeteries have granted use of land for interment of ashes. As in churchyards, special areas are being set aside for this purpose in cemeteries although lease periods are usually for periods longer than are granted in churchyards. Some cemeteries grant leases for as little as five years although normally the length of time is 25 years.

Most cemeteries allow headstones to be erected over the plots where ashes have been interred and some are additionally returning to the provision made in older cemeteries of buildings or rooms designed to store and show urns containing ashes. These columbaria have niches in their walls in which cremated remains are placed. In cemeteries too it is often possible to erect plaques on walls, giving the deceased's name and dates, around path edges or on plants or trees. Many crematoria, like many churches, have books of remembrance in which the names of those whose cremated remains are interred are recorded, often on separate pages for the date of death.

Other memorials

As alluded to above, some crematoria inter cremated remains not only in separate plots in lawns but also in flowerbeds and under trees. Ashes may be placed either under existing plants or trees or perhaps under those planted specifically to commemorate the deceased. Plaques, either on the plant or nearby, can be erected. Both crematoria and churches dedicate benches in memory of those whose ashes are interred nearby. Requests for such memorials are not always granted, however, as otherwise the churchyards, burial and crematoria grounds would be overrun with places to sit down!

Other types of memorials

For many generations of our forebears, the only way to remember a deceased loved one was to erect and then subsequently visit a grave. In our own age of fast and widespread communication memorialization could hardly be easier.

There are now a number of Internet websites that are dedicated to creating and preserving electronic memorials to loved ones. One of the oldest and most popular is run by a computer science teacher at the University of Newcastle – <http://catless.ncl.ac.uk/VMG>. At this Virtual Memorial Garden, visitors can find 'a place where people can celebrate their family, friends and pets and tell the rest of us about them and why they are special'. At another site – <www.cemetery.org> – visitors can post whole pages of memorials, including pictures and words, as well as text, for a one-off fee. Should you wish, you can even 'purchase' a star, which is then named after a loved one. <www.international-star-registry.org> is the site at which such memorials can be made (for a fee). The star map designation Hercules RA 16h 56m 32sd 38 long. 15 lat. is, for instance, named after a former police officer, Larry T. Young.

A less exotic form of memorial is to make some kind of charitable donation in memory of the loved one. Funeral directors will usually collect money given in memory of a particular person around the time of the funeral and will pass it on directly to the charity concerned. Normally undertakers will not charge for this service. A good way of advertising that you wish for money to be given to charity is to include notice of this in any obituary that is made in the press before the funeral. Remember that if the gift is made to a registered charity, tax payers can give money and, provided a Gift Aid declaration is signed (this simply says that the donor is a UK tax payer), the charity can claim the tax back from the government at no added cost to either themselves or the donor. This adds to the value of the donation. Some people, especially those who have been prominent in public life, may have a charity set up in their name after their death. This, though, will involve a lot of administration and is best done with the assistance of professionals in the field – accountants and solicitors.

Remembering

As well as gravestones described above (which are admittedly the more usual types of memorials) and the other kinds of memorials we have described, there are other helpful and popular ways of remembering a loved one. Many people, especially in the time immediately after a bereavement, find it helpful to make a scrapbook of their loved one's life. This can then be looked at in sad times by those left behind to help them cope with their loss. As well as including pictures and cuttings of the person's life, such a scrapbook can also include stories about the deceased and perhaps poems that have touched the heart of the person who is making the book (or even poems that they have themselves written about the deceased). Some people have also found it helpful to make a tape of favourites pieces of music, which either remind them of their loved one or which have helped them since the time of death. It might also be possible to make a video of clips of the person's life. This may be especially helpful if there is no grave to visit or little opportunity to make a physical expression of the loss that is felt (those who are housebound, for instance, may find this particularly helpful).

Whatever form of memorial you choose to make in memory of a loved one, or which you hope that others will make after your own death, it is important that you feel that the memorial is appropriate for you. Just as there is no such thing as the right way to grieve, neither is there any one right way to remember. Some find it helpful to talk to others about the deceased while others prefer to keep silent. While some find listening to sad songs to be unhelpful to them in remembering a loved one, others find that this brings comfort and peace. Whatever remembering is done, and whatever memorialization takes place as part of this, it should be real and helpful to those involved and should not be done simply as a result of the pressure of others or for the sake of doing what is seen to be right.

Notes

2 Funerals and Death

1 Douglas J. Davies, *Death, Ritual and Belief* (London, Cassell, 1997).
2 Davies, *Death*, pp. 27ff.
3 Davies, *Death*, p. 82. Davies is at this point summarizing J. P. Parry, *Death in Banaras* (Cambridge, Cambridge University Press, 1994).
4 Davies, *Death*, p. 83.
5 Richard Dawkins, 'Religion's Misguided Missiles', *Guardian*, 15 September 2001.

3 Christianity and Death

1 Keith Ward, *The Battle for the Soul* (London, Hodder & Stoughton, 1985), p. 152.
2 Jürgen Moltmann, *The Way of Jesus Christ: Christology in Messianic Dimensions* (London, SCM Press, 1990), pp. 254–6.

Glossary

Throughout this book we have tried to present the material relating to funerals and end-of-life decisions as clearly as we can while still explaining as fully as is possible all the complex choices that need to be made. There may be some words or phrases, however, that either we have used or are used by others or contained in their procedures and documents, which are unfamiliar to you. To help you through this particular maze of jargon, we have compiled below a list of specialized words used in this area and a brief explanation of their meanings.

Ashuary A place for the common burial of *cremated remains* after they have been kept for a period in a *vault* or *columbarium*.

Backfill To fill in and cover a *grave* with earth immediately after burial of a *coffin* or *casket*.

Bier A moveable frame on which a *coffin* or corpse stands before burial or cremation. Also the support for carrying a coffin or corpse to the *grave*.

Body stone A stone slab that completely covers the full length of a *grave*. It is gabled in shape or sometimes rounded.

Burial ground A wide-ranging term for a place of burial. It may be the ground around a church or chapel, a public area owned by a local council or a private area owned by a family or individual.

Casket A small box or chest, usually wooden, for cremated remains. In the USA the word is used to denote a *coffin* that has sides which are rectangular rather than tapered.

Catafalque A structure on which a *coffin* or corpse lies during a funeral service or a lying-in-state.

Cemetery A place used for burial, usually a large public area.

Cenotaph A monument to honour a person who is buried elsewhere. The word comes from Greek, literally meaning 'empty tomb'.

Chapel of rest Originally an *undertaker's mortuary*, the term now more generally means a place where a body is kept before a funeral and where it may be viewed. Used in such a way, chapels of rest exist in many hospitals.

Charnel house A place, especially a *vault*, where dead bodies or bones are piled and stored.

Chest tomb Sometimes called a box tomb, a stone or brick box built over a grave.

Churchyard An enclosed ground, surrounding a church, used for burial.

Coffin A box, usually made of wood but sometimes of metal, in which a corpse is buried or cremated.

Coffin-plate A plaque on the lid or foot end of a *coffin* detailing the name, dates and perhaps other information relating to the deceased.

Columbarium A place of storage with shelves or niches for caskets of ashes, which may either be on display or sealed with *plaques* marking individual plots.

Common grave A single place of burial of more than one corpse, usually without memorialization of individuals buried in the plot. These are to be found where warfare or widespread disease has led to a large number of people dying in a short period.

Consecrated ground A plot of land that has been dedicated and blessed by a bishop and which is set apart for the burial of the dead or their *cremated remains*.

Cremated remains The calcified remains of a body that has been cremated. These are usually passed through a *cremulator*.

Cremator A machine that cremates a *coffin* and corpse by means of flames and high temperature.

Crematory The place in a crematorium where the *cremators* are to be found.

Cremulator A machine that reduces the calcified remains of a body to a powder after cremation.

Deposition When used in relation to a corpse this is the act of burial in the ground or placement in a *mausoleum* or catacomb. When used in relation to *cremated remains* this may mean either the scattering of ashes, the interment of ashes or the placement in a *columbarium*, *mausoleum* or catacomb.

Disbursements The fees payable as part of a total funeral package, which are set by those other than the *funeral director* (minister's fee and crematorium fee, for instance).

Eulogy The homily or sermon given at a funeral, which speaks in praise of the departed.

Exhumation The removal from the ground of a corpse previously buried.

Faculty A legal document issued by the Church of England that allows for memorials to be placed in a church or *churchyard*, or for other changes to these places to be made.

Footstone A small, upright stone *memorial* set at the foot of a *grave* giving details of the deceased and perhaps other information, prose or poetry.

Funeral director An alternative, and increasingly common, name for an *undertaker*.

Funeral parlour The business premises of a *funeral director*.

Garden of Remembrance A piece of land, often adjoining a church or crematorium, which is set apart as a memorial to the departed. It may have individual or communal *memorials* giving the names of those being commemorated and may also be a piece of land in which ashes are interred.

Grave A place in the ground in which a corpse or corpses have been or are to be placed.

Gravestone A *memorial* placed on a *grave*. It may be either upright or placed flat on the grave.

Graveyard A plot of land adjacent to or belonging to a church or chapel that is used for the burial of corpses or *cremated remains*.

Headstone An upright stone *memorial* placed at the head of a *grave* with an inscription relating to the deceased.

Hearse A car or carriage used to carry a *coffin* at a funeral.

Inhumation The burial of a corpse, usually in a *coffin*, in the ground.

Interment The burial of a corpse or *cremated remains*, especially with prayers or other ceremony.

Kerbset The long pieces of stone that border a *grave*. They may surround turf and/or flowers, stone chippings or a body stone.

Landing stone The large piece of stone or concrete that is placed on the top of a *grave* to act as a base for a monument.

Ledger Also called a *body stone*, this is a piece of stone that totally covers a *grave*. It is also the term for the top of a *chest tomb*.

Lych gate A wooden, gable-roofed gate at the entrance to a *churchyard*. Originally these were used as a temporary shelter for the *bier* during a funeral and part of the funeral liturgy took place here.

Mausoleum A large and stately building designated as a place of burial or entombment of corpses or *cremated remains*, most often reserved for a particular family.

Memorial A wide-ranging term for a sign or monument to a deceased person or group of people.

Memorial garden A plot of land where either *cremated remains* are interred or where no ashes have been deposited but which nevertheless is set aside as a place for remembrance of the departed.

Monument A general term used to denote a structure or building erected to commemorate a dead person or group of people, or a particular event.

Mortuary A place where dead bodies are kept for a time, most often immediately prior to a funeral with attendant burial or cremation.

Ossuary *A vault* or other storage place for the common burial or storage of bones of the dead, i.e. another name for a *charnel house*.

Pall A large piece of heavy cloth, often made of velvet, which may be spread over a *coffin* at a funeral. Most often a pall is purple or black in colour (the colour of penitence and mourning) but sometimes it is white (signifying resurrection).

Pall-bearer A person who helps to carry (or, more properly 'shoulder') a *coffin* at a funeral.

Pascal candle A large candle, kept in many churches, which is first lit at Easter each year and also lit at services of baptism. It may stand alongside a *coffin* during a funeral as a reminder of the Christian faith into which the deceased had been baptized.

Pedestal tomb Similar to *chest tomb* but taller and narrower and not necessarily flat-topped.

Plaque An engraved tablet affixed to a wall or set into the ground, giving the names, dates and perhaps other details of the departed who are commemorated or interred in a *memorial garden* or *garden of remembrance*.

Sarcophagus A large stone *coffin*, often with additional sculpture or engravings.

Table tomb A raised *body stone*, which is held up at its four corners by small pillars, which themselves stand on a *landing stone*.

Tablet A small, flat slab of stone, metal or wood that has details of a deceased person or group of people, or event, inscribed upon it.

Tomb Used in two senses, to denote either a place of burial or the *monument* erected over the place of burial.

Tombstone Originally the stone cover of a *coffin*, the word is now more commonly used when talking of the large horizontal piece of stone covering a *grave* or a *memorial* over a tomb.

Undertaker A professional person whose business is to arrange funerals and their associated requirements, also known as a *funeral director*.

Urn Another, older, name for a casket that contains *cremated remains*. It is also the name for a piece of decoration found on some *monuments*, *headstones* or *memorials*.

Vault An enclosed chamber, usually underground, set aside for the burial or entombment of corpses or *cremated remains*.

Vigil From the Latin word meaning 'to watch', a vigil is the time before a funeral, usually the night before, when prayers and other devotions are said for the departed.

Wake A watch or *vigil*, most often held before a funeral, at which mourners share memories of the deceased.

Walled grave Although most *graves* are simply dug from the earth, the *coffin* is interred and the grave *backfilled*, some graves are lined with brick, stone or concrete. This may be so the grave is more easily opened up again for another, subsequent burial.

Useful Addresses

We have mentioned on a number of occasions throughout this book that many of the enquiries or questions you may have concerned with funerals and their arrangements will be easily dealt with by local funeral directors and clergy. If you are unclear about any of the issues dealt with in this book, or indeed about anything concerning funerals, please do not hesitate to contact them. However, if for some reason you require further information and advice the following list of agencies may prove to be useful.

Age Concern England

Astral House, 1268 London Road, Norbury, London SW16 4ER.
Tel: 020 8679 8000; e-mail: <age@ace.org.uk>;
website: <www.ace.org.uk>

Age Concern Northern Ireland

3 Lower Crescent, Belfast BT7 1NR.
Tel: 028 9024 5729.

Age Concern Scotland

113 Rose Street, Edinburgh EH2 3DT.
Tel: 0131 220 3345.

Age Concern Wales

4th floor, Cathedral Road, Cardiff CF1 9SD.
Tel: 029 2039 9562; e-mail: <accymru@ace.org.uk>

Useful Addresses

Alzheimer's Disease Society

Gordon House, 10 Greencoat Place, London SW1P 1PH.
Tel: 020 7306 0606.

Asian Family Counselling Service

76 Church Road, Hanwell, London W7 1LB.
Tel: 020 8567 5616.

Association of Burial Authorities

155 Upper Street, Islington, London N1 1RA.
Tel: 020 7288 2522.

Britannia Shipping Company (sea burials)

Britannia House, Newton Poppleford, Sidmouth,
Devon EX10 0EF.
Tel: 01395 568 652.

British Organ Donors' Society

Balsham, Cambridge CB1 6DL.
Tel: 01223 893 636; e-mail: <body@argonect.co.uk>;
website: <www.argonet.co.uk/body>

CancerLink

11–21 Northdown Street, Islington, London N1 9BN.
Tel: 020 7833 2818; Helpline: 0800 132905.

CancerLink (Scotland)

9 Castle Street, Edinburgh EH1 2DP.
Tel: 0131 228 5567; e-mail: <cancerlink@cislink.demon.co.uk>

Citizens' Advice Bureaux

See telephone directory for local details.

Commonwealth War Graves Commission

2 Marlow Road, Maidenhead, Berkshire SL6 7DX.
Tel: 01628 771208; website: <www.cwgc.org>

Compassionate Friends

53 North Street, Bristol BS3 1EN.
Tel: 0117 966 5202; Helpline: 0117 953 9639.

Cremation Society

2nd floor, Brecon House, 16 Albion Place, Maidstone,
Kent ME14 5DZ.
Tel: 01622 688 292.

CRUSE Bereavement Care

Cruse House, 126 Sheen Road, Richmond, Surrey TW9 1UR.
Tel: 020 8940 4818;
Helpline (Monday to Friday 9.30 a.m.–5 p.m.): 020 8332 7227.

Department of Social Security

See telephone directory for local details.

FACTS Health Centre (for those who have been bereaved by AIDS)

23–25 Weston Park, Crouch End, London N8 9SY.
Tel: 020 8348 9195.

Family Records Centre

1 Myddleton Street, London EC1R 1UW.
Tel: 020 8392 5300; certificate enquiries: 020 7233 9233;
website: <www.open.gov.uk/pro>

Federation of British Cremation Authorities

41 Salisbury Road, Carshalton, Surrey SM5 3HA.
Tel: 020 8669 4521.

Financial advice

Various websites including: <www.moneyextra.com>

Funeral Ombudsman

26–28 Bedford Row, London WC1R 4HE.
Tel: 020 7430 1112.

Funeral Planning Council

Melville House, 70 Drymen Road, Bearsden, Glasgow G61 2RP.
Tel: 0141 942 5885.

Funeral Standards Council

30 North Road, Cardiff CF1 3DY.
Tel: 029 2038 2046.

Help the Aged

St James's Walk, Clerkenwell Green, London EC1R 0BE.
Tel: 020 7253 0253;
Seniorline (Monday to Friday 9 a.m.–4 p.m.): 020 8800 6565.

Internet memorials

<http://catless.ncl.ac.uk/VMG>
<www.cemetery.org>
<www.international-star-registry.org>

Lesbian and Gay Bereavement Project

Vaughan Williams Centre, Colindale Hospital,
London NW9 5HG.
Tel: 020 8200 0511;
Helpline (Monday to Thursday 1.30 p.m.–5 p.m.): 020 8455 8894.

Macmillan Cancer Relief Fund

15–19 Britten Street, London SW3 3TZ.
Tel: 020 7351 7811.

Useful Addresses

National Association of Bereavement Services

20 Norton Folgate, London E1 6DB.
Tel: 020 7247 0617; Helpline: 020 7247 1080.

National Association of Funeral Directors

618 Warwick Road, Solihull, West Midlands B91 1AA.
Tel: 0121 711 1343.

National Association of Memorial Masons

27a Albert Street, Rugby, Warwickshire CV21 2SG.
Tel: 01788 542 264.

National Association of Widows

54–57 Allison Street, Digbeth, Birmingham B5 5TH.
Tel: 0121 643 8348.

Natural Death Centre

20 Heber Road, London NW2 6AA.
Tel: 020 8208 2853;
e-mail: <rhino@dial.pipex.com>;
website: <www.worldtrans.org/naturaldeath.html>

NHS Organ Donor Register

UK Transport Support Service Authority, Foxden Road, Stoke
Gifford, Bristol BS34 8RR.
Tel: 0117 975 7575;
website: <www.nhs.organdonor.net>

Office of Fair Trading

Field House, 15–25 Breams Buildings, London EC4A 1PR.
Tel: 020 7242 2858.

Parkinson's Disease Society

215 Vauxhall Bridge Road, London SW1V 1EG.
Tel: 020 7931 8080;
Helpline (Monday to Friday 10 a.m.–4 p.m.): 020 7269 8543.

Pensions Scheme Registry

PO Box 1NN, Newcastle upon Tyne NE99 1NN.
Tel: 0191 225 6394.

Registrar General for England and Wales

Smedley Hydro, Trafalgar Road, Birkdale, Southport PR8 2HH.
Tel: 0151 471 4200.

Registrar General for Guernsey

The Greffe, Royal Court House, St Peter Port,
Guernsey GY1 2PB.

Registrar General for the Isle of Man

Finch Road, Douglas, Isle of Man.

Registrar General for Northern Ireland

Oxford House, 49–55 Chichester Square, Belfast BT1 4HL.

Registrar General for the Republic of Ireland

Joyce House, 8–11 Lombard Street East, Dublin 2, Eire.

Registrar General for Scotland

New Register House, Edinburgh EN1 3YT.
Tel: 0131 334 0380.

Registry of Shipping and Seamen

PO Box 165, Cardiff CF4 5FU.
Tel: 029 2074 7333;
e-mail: <marine.informationcentre.msa.sp@gtnet.gov.uk>

Useful Addresses

Samaritans

10 The Grove, Slough, Berkshire SL1 1QP.
Tel: 01753 532713; Helpline: 08457 909 090;
e-mail: <jo@samaritans.org>;
website: <www.samaritans.org.uk>

Society of Allied and Independent Funeral Directors

Crowndale House, 1 Ferdinand Place, London NW1 8EE.
Tel: 020 7267 6777;
e-mail: <info@saif.org.uk>;
website: <www.saif.org.uk>

Superintendent Registrar for Jersey

State Offices, Royal Square, St Helier, Jersey JE1 1DD.

War Pensions Agency

Norcross, Blackpool FY5 3WP.
Tel: 01253 858 858.

The Woodland Trust

Ref. 1744, Freepost, Grantham, Lincolnshire NG31 6BR.
Tel: 01476 590808.

EE DCPL0000181328

941·58

=-MAR 2011

SOCIAL THOUGHT ON IRELAND IN THE

NINETEENTH CENTURY

CCOS JAN

Dedicated to the memory of
George Watson

*